WOMEN
OF THE BIBLE

The Victorious, the Victims, the Virtuous, and the Vicious

PETER DEHAAN, PHD

Women of the Bible: The Victorious, the Victims, the Virtuous, and the Vicious
Copyright © 2018, 2020 by Peter DeHaan.

Book 1 in the Bible Bios series. Second edition.

ISBN:
    978-1-948082-05-1 (ebook)
    978-1-948082-04-4 (paperback)
    978-1-948082-17-4 (hard cover)
    978-1-948082-51-8 (audiobook)

Published by Spiritually Speaking Publishing

Credits:
    Developmental editor: Margot Starbuck
    Copy editor/proofreader: Robyn Mulder
    Creative consultants: Cathy Rueter, James L. Rubart, and Rebekah Blomenberg
    Cover design: Sherwin Soy and Cassia Friello
    Author photo: Chele Reagh, PippinReaghDesign
    Audiobook narrator: James L. Rubart

To the women in my life: Bonnie DeHaan, Candy DeHaan, Laura Alexander, Kelli DeHaan, Abigail Alexander, and Kolby DeHaan.

Books by Peter DeHaan

Bible Bios series:

- *Women of the Bible: The Victorious, the Victims, the Virtuous, and the Vicious*

- *Friends and Foes of Jesus: Explore How People in the New Testament React to God's Good News*

52 Churches series:

- *52 Churches: A Yearlong Journey Encountering God, His Church, and Our Common Faith*

- *The 52 Churches Workbook: Becoming a Church that Matters*

- *More Than 52 Churches: The Journey Continues*

- *The More Than 52 Churches Workbook: Pursue Christian Community and Grow in Our Faith*

Dear Theophilus series:

- *Dear Theophilus: A 40-Day Devotional Exploring the Life of Jesus through the Gospel of Luke*

- *Dear Theophilus Acts: 40 Devotional Insights for Today's Church*

- *Dear Theophilus Isaiah: 40 Prophetic Insights about Jesus, Justice, and Gentiles*

- *Dear Theophilus Minor Prophets: 40 Prophetic Teachings about Unfaithfulness, Punishment, and Hope*

- *Dear Theophilus Job: 40 Insights About Moving from Despair to Deliverance*

Other books:

- *Jesus's Broken Church: Reimagine Our Sunday Traditions from a New Testament Perspective*

- *Woodpecker Wars: Celebrating the Spirituality of Everyday Life*

- *95 Tweets: Celebrating Martin Luther in the 21st Century*

- *How Big is Your Tent? A Call for Christian Unity, Tolerance, and Love*

Be the first to hear about Peter's new books and receive updates at www.PeterDeHaan.com/updates.

Contents

Introduction

Working on *Women of the Bible* has been a rewarding experience, far more than I could have imagined. Their lives are rich with beauty in both subtle and significant ways. I can't help but be affected. They move me profoundly. They touch me spiritually. Because of them I am in greater awe of God as I see the pious faith of most and the tragic failings of a few. My prayer is that, because of their example, both women and men will be encouraged and inspired.

My goal with *Women of the Bible* is to explore the lives of these remarkable biblical women. Through their stories we can better understand God and faith. While each entry focuses on one of them, some of their storylines overlap so we see them pop up again in other accounts, just like a good friend returning for a visit.

Here's some background information about *Women of the Bible*:

Even though these ladies lived long ago, I write about each in the present tense. This helps their stories come alive for us and reminds us that Scripture, though an ancient document, is relevant for us today.

I wish each woman had a different name, but not all do. For example, there are two Jezebels, two Sarahs, and two Susannas. There are three Deborahs and three Tamars. There are at least six Marys, possibly eight. Several less common names also repeat. In each case I added a number after their name to distinguish them (just like on IMDB for actors with the same name).

The ladies make their appearance in approximate chronological order, starting with Eve in Genesis and ending with Jezebel (2) in Revelation.

I used the Bible for my research. I didn't consult other historical documents or modern works, to avoid confusing the biblical story with other sources.

I tried to note each time I made reasonable assumptions about these women and their situations.

At the end of each section, I list the Bible passages that relate to each subject. If you're not used to reading the Bible, see "Bonus Material: For Those New to the Bible" for a quick overview.

Various translations of the Bible spell some names differently. *Women of the Bible* follows the spelling found in the New International Version (NIV). When needed, I consulted the New Jerusalem Bible. (See "Bonus Material: The Full Picture.")

Some women shared their names with men. Noah is one example. Yes, there is a woman named Noah in the Bible. She is one of Zelophehad's five daughters. In other instances, some women's names are also the names of cities, such as Maakah. In addition to there being six women named Maakah, there are two or three cities bearing that name, in addition to a couple of guys.

The section, "Bonus Material: For Further Study" lists even more biblical women not included in this book.

This book was a joy to research and write. I learned so much. Part of me is sad it's over. Another part of me is excited to finally share these words with you. I pray these women's lives will touch you as much as they touched me.

Let's Get Started

Some people—mostly those who know little about the Bible or have never actually read it—criticize its portrayal of women. They wrongly conclude that God dislikes females. This makes no sense because women are part of his amazing creation, made in his image. When he completes his work, he looks it over and is pleased with the results—all of it, including the woman he made.

While Scripture points us to God, the narrative takes place during a time when women are largely demeaned by the men who control society. This isn't God's plan. This is man's perversion of it—along with the help of contemptible Satan.

When we read the Bible with the understanding of the culture in which it takes place, we repeatedly see God's efforts to elevate women above the role mankind's sin forces them into. From the beginning of creation God intended men and women to complement each other and function as equals. A careful reading of Eve's story confirms this, a march through the Old Testament supports this, and the New Testament advances this.

We see this best by what happens after Jesus dies. His body goes missing. Angels task some women, specifically Mary Magdalene, to go tell the disciples Jesus is alive. This is significant, as a woman's testimony isn't legally accepted in that time and place. God has a different perspective. As if to underscore his affirmation of women, he has them deliver the breaking news of the most significant event in human history. This makes women the first apostles after Jesus's death—and the first missionaries.

As today's followers of God, we will do well to embrace what he desires: for women and men to complement each other and interact as equals. In considering these women in the Bible, we—both women and men—can learn much from them.

Through their example, we can:

Celebrate the Victorious: Some women in the Bible accomplish remarkable things and enjoy mighty victories. Consider Judge Deborah. She steps up to lead an army when a man refuses to. We commend her, and others like her, for her bravery and her faith. May we celebrate what these amazing women accomplished and be bold like them.

Affirm the Virtuous: Many of the women in the Bible are noteworthy for their goodness. I suspect there are more virtuous women in Scripture than virtuous men. Mary, the mother of Jesus, is an example of their righteousness. With a shortage of integrity in today's world, we can affirm the remarkable women in the Bible and strive to follow their virtuous examples. May we be more like them.

Mourn with the Victims: Sadly, some women in the Bible are victims. They suffer because of what others (usually men) do to them. Think about Jephthah's daughter, whose future is tragically altered after her dad makes a foolish vow to God. While many of the victims in the Bible maintain their virtue amid their circumstances and may even have a silent victory of sorts, we mostly mourn what happened to them. Their stories encourage us to fight injustice and restore the marginalized to their rightful place in society.

Avoid the Errors of the Vicious: Depraved behavior is not the sole domain of men. A few women in the Bible are likewise wicked. A notable example is Queen Jezebel, who personifies evil in all she does. Lacking any redeeming characteristics, Jezebel and other vicious women like her exemplify sin unchecked, providing examples of what we should avoid. We must do what we can to oppose such people and promote honest, honorable actions.

Some women transcend these four tidy categories, being virtuous while a victim or enjoying victory because of virtue. Other women don't quite fit in any of these four areas. Eve, the first woman, is one such example, and we'll start our exploration of biblical women with her.

WOMEN IN THE OLD TESTAMENT

Eve

Eve is a well-known biblical figure. Surprisingly, she's only mentioned by name four times in the Bible, twice in Genesis and twice in the New Testament. Sometimes called the mother of humanity, she is best known for picking the fruit God specifically prohibited—and giving some to her husband.

Eve often receives the heaviest criticism for disobeying God. Adam, however, is likewise culpable. He could have—and should have—put a stop to eating the forbidden fruit. More contemptible is the serpent, who lies to seduce Eve into disobeying God. Because of their actions, all three—Adam, Eve, and the serpent—suffer consequences, which they pass on to future generations, including ours.

Looking specifically at Eve, she receives three punishments for her disobedience: pain in childbirth, a desire to control her husband, and him ruling over her. So before Adam and Eve messed up, we can assume things must have been the opposite for women: childbirth would have been easy, women did not seek to control their husbands, and men did not rule over their wives.

The judgment Eve receives transfers forward to future generations, with women trying to control men and men wanting to rule women. However, in the beginning there is neither controlling nor ruling. There is equality, with God intending men and women to live as equals.

Do we try to control those around us? Do we let others rule over us? How might God want us to change?

[Discover more about Eve in Genesis 2–4, 2 Corinthians 11:3, and 1 Timothy 2:13.]

Adah (1) and Zillah

Lemech is the first polygamist in the Bible. His two wives are Adah and Zillah. Adah has two sons: Jabal and Jubal. Zillah also has a son, Tubal-Cain, as well as a daughter, Naamah (1).

Though Adah and Zillah must share their husband's affections, there's no mention of strife between them. This is not the case for most of the other polygamist marriages that follow it in Scripture. Having multiple wives is certainly different than God's idea of two people joining to become one.

From what we know, however, Adah and Zillah get along. This is a tribute to them and their character. They must make an intentional effort to live together in harmony. For them, having the same husband is the highest level of sharing.

It's not fair that they need to divvy up the attention of one man, and doing so is not God's intent. However, they do what they need to do to make their situation work and avoid contention.

When we find ourselves in an unfair circumstance outside of our control, do we work to make the best of it or show our displeasure by causing problems for everyone around us?

[Discover more about Adah and Zillah in Genesis 4:19–23, along with Genesis 2:24.]

The Wife of Noah

What would you do if your best friend or your spouse came to you and said, "God spoke to me. He told me to do something that doesn't make sense and will take a long time"? Would you stand by that person? Would you support him or her?

This is the position Noah's wife finds herself in. God tells Noah to build a huge boat, big enough for animals to live on, along with enough food to sustain them. He says there will be a flood, and everyone and everything not on the boat will die.

However, there's no water nearby. Everyone laughs. They mock Noah for being foolish. Surely, he's crazy. From everyone's perspective, she's married to a madman, one who claims to hear from God and persists in doing something audacious.

This goes on for years, one hundred years. Surely friends and neighbors ostracize them. Not only must they work hard to build their boat, but I'm sure they do so in isolation.

The Bible doesn't tell us if Noah's wife supports him or not, but since she's allowed to go on the boat and be saved from drowning, it's likely she stood by her man despite what others thought, said, or did. That's loyalty. That's commitment.

She's an example for us all to follow.

How loyal are we to our spouse, family, and friends? Do we need to make any changes?

[Discover more about Noah's wife in Genesis 5–9, specifically Genesis 5:32, Genesis 6:10, 18, Genesis 7:7, 13, and Genesis 8:16.]

The Daughters-In-Law of Noah

Like Noah's wife, we know little of Noah's three daughters-in-law and can only speculate from their story in the Bible. Like their mother-in-law, we can reasonably assume they each stand by their men, supporting them in their questionable ark-constructing business and helping them to build the gigantic boat. They, too, endure hardship, ridicule, and isolation as the people around mock and shun them.

When the flood comes, they get on the boat and live. Everyone else dies. All that's left in the world are eight people, only four couples. Just like Eve and her husband, God tells these three women and their husbands to be fruitful and multiply. It's a do-over for humanity, Creation 2.0.

From these three women come all future generations. The human race is saved. Nations form.

Though nameless, these three women give birth to the future of civilization. We are here today because of them.

Even if we remain nameless, what are we giving birth to? What are we making today for the generations of tomorrow?

[Discover more about Noah's three daughters-in-law in Genesis 5–9, specifically Genesis 9:1, 7, 19, along with Genesis 1:22, 28.]

The Wife of Job

Through no fault of Job, Satan attacks him, wiping away his wealth and killing all his children. Next, Satan afflicts Job's health, leaving him in agony. The suffering man wishes he were dead, that he'd never been born. All Job has left is his life, four unsupportive friends, and a wife who harasses him. Job may have been better off without her.

As Job struggles to maintain his faith in God and hold on to his righteousness, Job's wife could choose to support him. She should be encouraging. Instead she turns on him. She ridicules his integrity and suggests he just curse God so he can die.

Job does not waver. He calls her foolish and does not sin. God spares Job and restores what Satan took from him.

Do we encourage those closest to us when they go through tough times, or do we make things even harder for them?

[Discover more about Job's wife in Job 1–2 and Job 42, especially Job 2:9–10.]

The Daughters of Job

After Satan's tormenting of the innocent Job, God restores what Satan took away, which includes all his possessions and his first set of seven sons and three daughters. In fact, God doubles Job's wealth and gives him ten more kids: seven more sons and three more daughters. Though the sons' names aren't recorded in Scripture, the daughter's names are: Jemimah, Keziah, and Keren-Happuch. The girls are heralded as the most beautiful in the land.

In mentioning them by name, the Bible honors Job's girls, even at the risk of elevating them over their unnamed brothers. Even more so, Job goes against the conventional practice of the day, giving his daughters an inheritance along with their brothers.

In doing so, Job reveals his heart and God's perspective. This is even more remarkable, given that Job lives in a male-dominated society.

May we see things as God sees them. What might we do to further God's perspective, even if it means challenging the status quo?

[Discover more about Job's three daughters in Job 42:13–15.]

The Wife of Lot

After Lot and Abraham go their separate ways, Lot eventually moves to the city of Sodom. God is displeased with the great sin of the people who live there, and he plans to destroy the city and its inhabitants. However, two angels go there first to rescue Lot and his family.

The next day, at dawn, the angels drag Lot, his wife, and his two daughters out of the city. As soon as they get out, the angels tell them to run for their lives, to not stop, and to not look back.

As they flee, Lot's wife can't help herself. She looks back at what they are leaving behind. When she does, she dies, turning into a pillar of salt.

Jesus mentions Lot's wife when he talks about the coming kingdom of God. He effectively says, look forward to what will be. Don't look back at what you're leaving behind.

Don't be like Lot's wife.

When we follow Jesus, do we look ahead to what he offers or long for the old life we left behind?

[Discover more about Lot's wife in Genesis 19:15–16, 26 and Luke 17:30–32.]

The Daughters of Lot

Lot has a creepy relationship with his daughters. He isn't a good dad. I feel sorry for his girls.

First, when the inhospitable men of Sodom rush Lot's house to have sex with the two men (actually angels) staying there, Lot tries to reason with them. He protects the angels and begs the townsmen not to pursue their wicked desires. As an alternative, he offers them his two virgin daughters to molest. How could a father even think of doing such a despicable thing? Fortunately for the girls, the townsmen aren't interested.

A loving dad would never consider offering his daughters to satisfy men's depravity. What did Lot's daughters think about their father after his cavalier dismissal of their chastity? What did his actions say about his view of their value as females? How could they maintain any self-worth?

Later, we find Lot and his daughters hunkered in a cave, isolated from other people. He's getting old. There are no men in sight, and the girls' biological clocks are ticking. Desperate, they concoct a heinous plan. On successive nights, they get their dad drunk and sleep with him. Both get pregnant and each give birth to a son.

While we can blame the girls for their depravity, I accuse Lot and his bad parenting as the primary offender. He shows his moral failings by offering up his daughters for sex, and they likely form their moral compass from his actions. Through this he effectively communicates their prime value is for sex. They merely seek to live out what he expects.

True, the girls are not innocent for their actions, but Lot could have produced a different outcome had he been a better father.

What kind of influence do we have on those around us?

[Discover more about Lot's two daughters in Genesis 19:4–38.]

Sarah (1)

The story of Sarah (first called Sarai) is scattered throughout the narrative in Genesis chapters 11 through 23. Not only is she the first wife of Abraham, she is also his half sister. Though this makes us squirm today, at the time, a man marrying his half sister isn't prohibited.

Sarah, whose name means *princess*, is most attractive. Abraham worries that would-be suitors will kill him to get her, so he asks her to say she is his sister. He even says this will be an act of love. She agrees and does so—twice—with other men taking her as their wife. Both times God protects Sarah and works out her return to Abraham, but what torment she must go through when they take her away, and Abraham does nothing to stop them.

Although God repeatedly promises Abraham children, Sarah grows tired of waiting. In her old age she concocts a plan where Abraham can have his promised child through her servant, Hagar. It's an ill-conceived idea, and Abraham is boneheaded for going along with it. Conflict results.

Later God confirms that Abraham's chosen child will come from Sarah. She laughs at this improbable promise, and God criticizes her for it. A year later, the child is born when Sarah is ninety and Abraham is one hundred. They name him Isaac, which means *laughter* or *he laughs*.

Sarah lives another thirty-seven years and dies at age 127.

With God, all things are possible, even a ninety-year-old woman having a baby or living 127 years.

Do we ever get tired of waiting for God and mess up his plans by doing things our way?

[Discover more about Sarah in Genesis 11–23, specifically Genesis 20:12 and Genesis 21:1–7.]

Hagar

Hagar is the Egyptian slave of Sarah. She is likely acquired during Abraham and Sarah's trip to Egypt during a famine. They could have avoided so much pain had they not bought her—or used better judgment afterward. Here's her story.

Sarah has no children, which she blames on God. She's well past her childbearing years. Sarah thinks she can vicariously have a family through Hagar, so Sarah offers her slave to Abraham to make a baby. This is a bad idea on Sarah's part, yet Abraham accepts it.

Hagar does become pregnant by Abraham. Though they never marry, the Bible later refers to Hagar as Abraham's wife. Being able to give Abraham what Sarah could not, Hagar looks down on Sarah, who blames Abraham for the whole mess. Wanting to avoid conflict, Abraham tells Sarah to handle it.

Sarah mistreats Hagar, who runs away. Alone in the desert, God's angel sends Hagar back, promising that her descendants will be too numerous to count. Hagar obeys God and soon Ishmael is born.

For about fourteen years things are okay for Hagar and Ishmael, but then Sarah becomes pregnant in her old age and gives birth to Isaac. Now Abraham has two sons, from two women.

Ishmael taunts the younger Isaac. Again, Sarah demands that Abraham fix the problem. This troubles Abraham, but God tells him to follow Sarah's wishes, for Abraham's legacy will come through Isaac, not Ishmael. Abraham sends Hagar and Ishmael off into the desert with some food and water. When their supplies are gone, they sit down in the wilderness to die.

But God does not abandon them, promising Hagar that her son will become a great nation. Then God shows her water. While this is the last we hear about Hagar, we know Ishmael lives to be 137, and he and Isaac eventually reconnect.

Hagar is a powerless victim who has no say over what Abraham and Sarah do to her. Nonetheless, God protects her. He cares for her, and her descendants are numerous, like a great nation.

God cares for the powerless. How can we help?

[Discover more about Hagar in Genesis 16 and Genesis 21.]

Rebekah

The family tree of Rebekah is confusing. She is the daughter-in-law of Abraham and Sarah, as well as their great niece (she is the daughter of their nephew, Bethuel; Abraham and Sarah share the same father.) That means Rebekah's great aunt and uncle are also her in-laws.

Abraham doesn't want his son Isaac marrying a local girl, so he sends his servant to his home country to find a bride for Isaac. With God's provision, the servant finds Rebekah—when she offers to water his camels—and she agrees to go with him to marry a man (and a relative) she has never met. This is a tribute to her character—or perhaps a reflection of her desire to leave home and marry. Isaac is forty, but we don't know Rebekah's age.

Just like her mother-in-law, Rebekah is beautiful. And just like his father, Isaac passes her off as his sister, a bad lesson he learned from his parents.

It takes twenty years for Rebekah to have children, but when she does, she has twins. While Isaac favors the older, Esau, Rebekah favors the younger, Jacob. When parents play favorites, it's never good. The boys don't get along and conflict ensues. When Esau threatens to kill Jacob, Rebekah feigns that she doesn't want Jacob to marry a local girl, hoping Isaac will send him back to their homeland. Isaac does.

So Rebekah is a beautiful woman of character, who (along with her husband) isn't such a good parent. May we not repeat their errors.

What character traits have we picked up from our parents that might cause us problems? If we have children, what are we modeling for them?

[Discover more about Rebekah in Genesis 24–28.]

Deborah (1)

When Rebekah agrees to leave home to marry Isaac, her family sends her off, along with her nurse. This suggests Rebekah may be quite young at the time and still in need of guidance. We later learn the nurse's name is Deborah, but we know nothing more about her or what she does.

However, the Bible does mention Deborah's death. We don't know why, but it must have been important for God to note her passing in his written Word.

Whether our life is celebrated, receives a mere footnote in history, or is soon forgotten, what we do is important to God.

Do we do things to get the world's attention or is God's opinion what matters most?

[Discover more about Deborah in Genesis 24, specifically verse 59, and Genesis 35:8.]

Rachel

Rachel is Jacob's second—and favorite—wife. She is also his first cousin. (Her father, Laban, and his mother, Rebekah, are brother and sister.)

Rachel is a shepherdess. Her story starts when Jacob's parents send him to their home country to find a wife from his mother's family. It must be love at first sight, for when he sees Rachel, he cries and kisses her. She's beautiful, and Jacob falls in love. Though they do get married, her dad first marries off her older sister Leah to Jacob. The sisters become co-wives, forever vying for their husband's affections.

Though Jacob loves Rachel more than Leah, it's Leah who has kids, while Rachel struggles with infertility. Rachel becomes jealous of her sister. Morality aside, this is a practical reason not to have multiple wives, especially those who are sisters.

In desperation, Rachel offers her maidservant to Jacob to produce children in her place. Jacob should have known better than to accept this, especially seeing how badly it worked out for his grandmother, Sarah, when she did this with Abraham.

Escalating the competition, Leah then does the same thing, offering her maidservant to Jacob to produce more children as her proxy.

Later, in a move reminiscent of Esau trading his birthright to Jacob for food, Rachel trades a night with her husband for some mandrakes, a plant believed to have magical powers, possibly including fertility. Ironically, while Rachel pursues magic to get pregnant, Jacob plants a seed in Leah for another child.

God eventually answers Rachel's prayers for a son, and Joseph is born. Then Rachel asks God for another boy. Tragically, she dies giving birth to her second son, Benjamin.

Though a beautiful woman with a loving husband, Rachel's life is filled with conflict and in wanting what she doesn't have.

Are we happy with what God gives us or do we desire more? When in conflict, do we escalate the situation, like Rachel and Leah, or seek peace?

[Discover more about Rachel in Genesis 29–31 and Genesis 35.]

Leah

Leah, like her younger sister, Rachel, is an interesting character. While Rachel is most attractive, Leah isn't. It's Rachel Jacob wants to marry, but Rachel's father pawns off Leah on Jacob instead. When Jacob complains, he's given Rachel too. So the two sisters go from vying for their father's attention to competing with one another for their husband's time.

Jacob loves Rachel but not Leah—though not so much that he won't sleep with her. Because she's unloved, God blesses her with children. First there's Reuben, then Simeon, followed by Levi and Judah.

Later, in a most unusual story, Leah gives Rachel some mandrakes, a plant believed to have magical powers, in exchange for a night with their joint husband. Leah gets pregnant again and has Issachar and later Zebulun. After that she has Dinah.

Rachel is jealous of her older sister. As the sisters compete for Jacob's attention, they introduce their handmaids into the marriage bed. Both maids produce two sons for Jacob.

After all this, Rachel has Joseph, and much later she dies giving birth to Benjamin. At last, it seems, Leah will not need to compete with her sister for Jacob's attention. But the reminder of Rachel forever looms, with Jacob showing favoritism to Rachel's sons, Joseph and Benjamin, over Leah's.

Leah is pawned off by her father to marry a man who doesn't want her, but God cares for her, blessing her with many children and a long life.

Family relationships are sometimes unfair and can cause hurt. Do we work to make things easier for our family or more difficult?

[Discover more about Leah in Genesis 29–30, Genesis 35:16–19, Genesis 37:3, and Genesis 42:4.]

Zilpah and Bilhah

Zilpah and Bilhah aren't familiar women in the Bible, yet their contribution to the nation of Israel is significant.

When Laban's two daughters marry Jacob, Dad gives them each a wedding gift: a servant. To his daughter Leah, he gives his servant Zilpah, while to his daughter Rachel, he gives Bilhah. These servants should be nothing more than a footnote in history, but that's not how the story unfolds. Their lives have a distressing parallel to Hagar who preceded them.

While Leah gives Jacob several sons, Rachel has no children. In desperation, she offers her servant, Bilhah, to her husband to make babies in her place. Her foolish husband agrees, impregnating his wife's servant—twice.

Not to be outdone, Leah does the same thing, offering her servant, Zilpah, to sleep with Jacob. Zilpah also gets pregnant—twice. Eventually Rachel has two boys of her own, while Leah has six sons altogether.

As a result, the two servants produce four sons for Jacob. Of his twelve boys, four are not from his wives, but from his wives' servants. The twelve boys become the twelve tribes of Israel (Jacob), so one third of the nation of Israel results from Jacob's relationship with his wives' two servants.

Zilpah and Bilhah have nothing to say in any of this. As servants, they must obey their mistresses. They are voiceless victims. But as he often does, God rewards the underdogs, with Zilpah and Bilhah's offspring comprising one third of his chosen people.

Even when we feel like helpless, voiceless victims, God is on our side. Do we truly believe that?

[Discover more about Zilpah and Bilhah in Genesis 29–35.]

Dinah

Dinah is the only daughter of Jacob and Leah. She is born after Zebulun, son #10, and before Joseph, son #11. Tragically, Shechem, a Hivite prince, rapes her. After his act of lust, he falls in love with her, offering whatever dowry her family asks. He demands his father make this happen.

Jacob fails to respond to his daughter's rape. We don't know if he's afraid or waiting for his sons to help avenge her dishonor. Regardless, Dinah's brothers are outraged when they hear what happened and immediately come home.

While her father fails to act, two of Dinah's brothers, Simeon and Levi, do. They retaliate without Jacob's knowledge. After killing Shechem and all the men of the village, they liberate their sister and leave. Was this revenge, a rescue, or both?

When her other brothers see that everyone in the town is dead, they plunder it.

Although Jacob criticizes Simeon and Levi for their excessive reaction and the subsequent risk to the entire family—should neighboring towns take revenge—they feel justified in avenging their sister's rape, despite the risk of retaliation.

After her rescue, we hear nothing more about Dinah. The end to her story is for us to ponder. Though we know what happens to Dinah and what happens because of her, we know nothing about what she says, does, or thinks. Though she's the center of action in this story, she plays a minor role.

When we encounter injustice, how do we respond? Over-reacting may be as bad as not reacting at all.

[Discover more about Dinah in Genesis 34.]

Tamar (1)

Tamar's a victim who takes extreme action to vindicate herself. She's the daughter-in-law of Judah, suffers at his hand, responds with guile, and has twins with him. Talk about a messed-up situation. But she's also one of four women mentioned in Jesus's family tree. Here's her story:

Tamar marries Judah's oldest son. He's evil, and God kills him. As is the custom of the day, she's passed on to his brother, her brother-in-law, so she can have kids through him. In this way he will produce children in his dead brother's place and perpetuate his brother's line as a surrogate husband. But the brother doesn't cooperate and with selfish intent refuses to impregnate her. This displeases God, and he kills the second brother too. As customary, Judah promises Tamar his third son when he's old enough and sends her back to her parents to wait. But Judah has no intention of following through, for he fears this son may die too.

Once Tamar realizes Judah will not do as he promised, she disguises herself as a prostitute. She waits where she knows Judah will pass. Not realizing who she is, he solicits her, leaving his seal and its cord, along with his staff as his pledge of payment. Tamar gets pregnant.

When Judah sends a friend to pay the prostitute and reclaim his pledge, the friend can't find her and no one in the area knows of a prostitute working there. Judah doesn't pursue the matter further.

Three months later Judah learns his daughter-in-law is expecting a child conceived out of wedlock, from an act of prostitution. With self-righteous indignation, he condemns her to die. Then she reveals he's the father and offers proof, by showing his seal, cord, and staff. Judah confesses his role, and he declares Tamar as more righteous than he.

Tamar has twins: Perez and Zerah. Judah, Tamar, and Perez are all ancestors of Jesus, and Matthew lists her in the genealogy of Jesus, one of only four women so honored.

Judah does Tamar wrong, first for promising his third son to her and not following through, then for using her as a prostitute, and last for condemning her to die. Yet Tamar also does wrong, posing as a harlot and soliciting her father-in-law to trap him. Neverthe-less, Tamar's drastic steps ensure she has a family to care for her when she gets old. And God ensures she has a legacy.

Do two wrongs make a right? When we are wronged, may we have the wisdom to know the right answer.

[Discover more about Tamar in Genesis 38:6–30, Ruth 4:12, and Matthew 1:3.]

The Wife of Potiphar

Through a series of events outside of his control, Joseph becomes a slave owned by Potiphar, one of Pharaoh's officials, who is captain of the guard. Joseph proves himself to the captain, who eventually puts his entire estate under his slave's care. Potiphar's household prospers because of Joseph's diligent work.

Joseph's a good-looking guy, and Potiphar's wife notices. We don't know if her husband ignores her, if she's bored, or if she's simply promiscuous, but she pursues Joseph. She tries to seduce him. He resists. He explains why he won't sleep with her, but she ignores his words, focusing only on her desire for his body.

This goes on day after day.

Joseph does his best to stay away from her. But one day as he goes about his work, she realizes no one else is around. She becomes aggressive, grabbing him and drawing him toward her. He pulls away, leaving his jacket in her hands as he flees.

Failing to satisfy her desires, her lust turns to revenge. She calls in her servants, spinning lies about Joseph, of how he went after her, of how she screamed for help, and of how he fled. She holds up his jacket as proof. When Potiphar gets home, she repeats her lies to him. In a rage, he throws Joseph in prison, where he languishes for years.

Potiphar's wife is an unfaithful spouse and an immoral woman who makes no effort to control her sexual desires. And when she can't seduce Joseph or even force him to sleep with her, she uses her position to destroy him.

How far are we willing to go to get what we want, even when it's wrong? How low will we stoop to hurt those who get in our way?

[Discover more about Potiphar's wife in Genesis 39:1–20.]

Asenath

Pharaoh later gives Joseph a wife. Her name is Asenath, and she is the daughter of the priest Potiphera. This is likely a strategic move, in hopes that Asenath will influence Joseph to accept Egyptian ways and beliefs. In this way, the king uses her as his pawn. He expects her to influence her husband for her country. She has no say in his plan.

Though we know Joseph is attractive and powerful, he's also an outsider, not even allowed to eat at the same table as the Egyptians. Asenath is forced to marry a foreigner. There is no hint of love or affection between the two. Though this could be a good life for her, it's surely not the life she wanted.

Asenath and Joseph have two sons, Manasseh and Ephraim. The descendants of each boy become tribes of Israel and receive an allotment of territory in the Promised Land. We know nothing else of the relationship between Asenath and Joseph. We don't know if he influences her to embrace God or not, but in looking at the life of Joseph, we see no hint that she distracts him from his faith or causes him to embrace her people's way of life.

When others try to use us, do we become their pawn or make our own path?

[Discover more about Asenath in Genesis 41:45, 50 and Genesis 46:20.]

Shiphrah and Puah

Shiphrah and Puah are Hebrew midwives at the time when the Israelites are enslaved in Egypt. Fearing their slaves' mounting numbers, the king of Egypt tells Shiphrah and Puah to kill all the baby Israelite boys as they are being born. But they fear God more than Egypt's pharaoh, so they disregard the king's order.

God honors them for their integrity and rewards them with their own families. Sometimes doing the right thing means disobeying human authority and manmade laws. God may honor us as a result, but we could also suffer the consequences for our actions.

Regardless of the outcome, are we willing to do what is right?

[Discover more about Shiphrah and Puah in Exodus 1:15–21.]

Jochebed

The Egyptians fear the mushrooming population of the enslaved Israelites and command all the Israelite baby boys be thrown into the Nile River. However, one mother sees something special in her baby and hides him for several months. When she can conceal him no longer, she does indeed put him in the Nile River but not before protecting him in a watertight basket. Then she strategically places the basket where a compassionate person might find him. The woman's daughter hides nearby to see what happens to her baby brother.

When the pharaoh's daughter comes to the river to bathe, she discovers the baby and wants to keep him as her own. The baby's sister steps out of hiding and offers to find a woman to nurse him. She gets her mother. Although the boy should die, the pharaoh's daughter saves him and even pays his biological mother to feed and care for him.

When the baby is weaned, his mother gives him back to the pharaoh's daughter—who names him Moses.

This mother's name is Jochebed and she has two other children, Aaron and Miriam.

Jochebed, like many moms, sees promise in her son and takes extraordinary measures to protect him so he can reach his potential.

Who has seen promise in us and made a difference in our lives? Who can we help reach their potential?

[Discover more about Jochebed in Exodus 2:1–10, Exodus 6:20, and Numbers 26:59.]

The Daughter of Pharaoh (1)

Pharaoh is not a name but a title for the king in Egypt. Therefore, there are many Pharaohs in the Bible and many daughters of Pharaoh. The first daughter of Pharaoh we encounter adopts baby Moses.

She finds him floating in the Nile River. Though she realizes he is a Hebrew baby and should be killed, she doesn't turn him over. Instead, she keeps him as her own child. She unwittingly pays his biological mother to nurse him, and when he is weaned she receives him back. She names him Moses, which means that she pulled him from the water.

We don't know if she is a good mom or not, though when Moses is older, he doesn't want to be called the son of the pharaoh's daughter. What we do know about her, however, is she is compassionate. Her actions save Moses and give the Hebrew people a leader to rescue them.

Do we live lives marked with compassion?

[Discover more about Pharaoh's daughter in Exodus 2:5–10, Acts 7:21, and Hebrews 11:24.]

Zipporah

With the pharaoh out to get him, Moses flees for his life. He marries the shepherdess Zipporah, daughter of the priest of Midian. They have two sons: Gershom and Eliezer.

Years later when Moses and his family travel to Egypt, God afflicts Moses. This is apparently because Moses has not circumcised his son Gershom, as God commanded the Israelites to do through Abraham.

Just as God is about to kill Moses for his disobedience, Zipporah takes decisive action. She whips out a knife, circumcises Gershom, and touches Moses with the removed foreskin. This appeases God, and he spares Moses.

Zipporah does what her husband did not do, she obeys God's command, and saves her husband's life.

Sometimes we must act when others fail to. How can we know when to act and when to wait?

[Discover more about Zipporah in Exodus 2:15–22, Exodus 4:24–26, and Exodus 18:2–6.]

Miriam

Miriam is the older sister of Moses. She's also the sister of Aaron. At the time when Moses is born, there's a decree to kill all baby boys. His mom hides him as long as she can. Then she puts him in a basket and places him in the Nile River.

Miriam watches at a distance to see what happens. When the pharaoh's daughter finds him, Miriam pops up and offers to find a woman to nurse him. She picks her mom.

Later, as an adult, Miriam is a prophet and worship leader. She directs the Israelite women in song and dance to celebrate God's rescue after they cross the sea to escape the pursuing Egyptian army.

Unfortunately, what we know best about Miriam as an adult is when she and Aaron oppose Moses out of jealousy, criticizing his choice for a wife. God's judgment is quick, instantly afflicting her with leprosy, a contagious skin disease, which is untreatable at the time. Though Aaron is also at fault, he is not so stricken, suggesting that Miriam led their tiny rebellion. When Aaron sees what happened to his sister, he immediately admits his bad attitude and begs Moses to intervene. Moses does, and God heals her.

A few years later Miriam dies. There's no mention of the people mourning her death, a sad end to a once-promising life. Though Miriam starts well as a brave and obedient daughter and later as a prophet and worship leader, she lets jealousy define her later life. God is not pleased.

What can we do to finish strong?

[Discover more about Miriam in Exodus 1–2, Exodus 15:20–21, Numbers 20:1, and Numbers 26:59.]

Kozbi

The nation of Israel has a problem. Many of their men are involved with women from Moab, indulging themselves sexually with these foreigners, something the Law of Moses prohibits. Then these women entice the men to go to church with them, where they offer sacrifices to Baal and worship him. Instead of God, the Israelites align themselves with Baal. God is not pleased. Moses orders the execution of each man who has strayed.

During all this, another man brings a Midianite woman into camp and into his tent. Her name is Kozbi. We don't know if he thinks this is okay because she is a Midianite and not a Moabite. Perhaps he wants to make a point or maybe he isn't thinking at all. We also don't know if Kozbi is aware of the situation or not. What we do know is that this man flaunts his sexual relationship with a foreign woman, a liaison God forbids and for which many other men have just died.

Phinehas, the priest, takes judgment into his hands in the form of a spear. He goes into the tent and drives the shaft all the way through the man and into Kozbi. This appeases God's wrath.

While Kozbi may have instigated this, it's more likely she is merely a naïve girl who ends up in the wrong situation. She pays for her ignorance with her life.

Being unaware is no excuse for doing wrong. There will still be consequences for our actions.

How willing are we to do what God says to do?

[Discover more about Kozbi in Numbers 25:1–18.]

The Daughters of Zelophehad

Zelophehad has five daughters but no sons. His girls are Mahlah, Noah, Hoglah, Milkah (2), and Tirzah. Zelophehad dies in the desert before he can receive his allotment of property in the Promised Land. Since he has no sons to receive his inheritance in his stead, the girls will get nothing.

They boldly go before Moses and ask for their father's share, contrary to convention. God tells Moses to include them in the land assignments, which Joshua later carries out.

With a population of millions, there are surely other daughters in this same predicament. But only these sisters come forward, and only these women receive land.

Are we willing to speak up to receive what is due us? Will we trust God with the outcome?

[Discover more about Zelophehad's five daughters in Numbers 26:33, Numbers 27:1–7, Numbers 36:1–11, Joshua 17:3–7, and 1 Chronicles 7:15.]

Rahab

Rahab is a prostitute two spies stay with when they scope out Jericho. We don't know if they seek her for her services or merely for a place to hide from public view.

Hearing of their presence, the king of Jericho commands Rahab to turn over the two men. Instead, in an act of treason, she hides them and lies to the king, saying they already left, but she doesn't know where they went.

Rahab knows God favors Israel and will give the city to them. In exchange for protecting the spies, she asks for her family's safety. As she lists who's included, she mentions parents and siblings, but no husband or children.

Joshua confirms that Rahab and her family will be spared when the city is conquered. After the people of Jericho are all killed, Rahab lives with the Israelites.

In the New Testament, Matthew reveals that Rahab is one of Jesus's direct ancestors and the great-great-grandmother of King David. She's honored as only one of four women mentioned in Jesus's family tree. Further, she's affirmed as a person of faith, one of only two women included in the Hebrews 11 "hall of fame." Finally, James confirms Rahab is righteous because of her courageous actions in protecting the two spies.

While our reaction may be to judge Rahab for her profession, God sees her differently, as a righteous woman of faith, and he rewards her accordingly.

How can we avoid judging others and instead see people as God sees them?

[Discover more about Rahab in Joshua 2, Joshua 6, Matthew 1:5, Hebrews 11:31, and James 2:25.]

Aksah

Caleb is one of the twelve spies sent to scope out the land the nation of Israel plans to conquer, but he is only one of two men who bring back a positive report. For his ability to look beyond the strength of the peoples they need to overcome and for his confidence in God's ability to provide, he is assured a reward when the people take the land.

When they arrive, Caleb pledges to give his daughter Aksah in marriage to whoever captures the city of Kiriath Sepher. Othniel, who is also Caleb's nephew, is up to the challenge, and he succeeds. As promised, Caleb awards Aksah to Othniel, and the pair marry. Aksah and Othniel are first cousins.

Although we may be dismayed that Caleb offers his daughter as a prize, we can also see Aksah as a cherished woman, both by her father and the man who strives to win her. Sometimes things are a matter of perspective.

What we might see as bad can also be good. Do we see things in a positive light or a negative one?

[Discover more about Aksah in Joshua 15:16–17, Judges 1:12–13, and 1 Chronicles 2:49.]

Deborah (2)

Though called a judge, Deborah is primarily a prophetess, a person who hears from God and proclaims his words to others. She is the only female judge in the Bible.

Deborah receives a prophetic message for Barak.

Through her, God commands him to raise an army and attack their enemy. God even promises that Barak will prevail, but he balks. He won't do it unless Deborah goes with him. She consents. However, she prophesies that because of his reluctance, the honor of killing the enemy's leader, Sisera, will go to a woman. While we may assume this woman is Deborah, it's another woman, Jael. Even so, Deborah receives more credit than Barak for the victory.

Deborah lives in a male-dominated society. Yet, when a man doesn't do what he is supposed to, she steps forward and acts. We commend her for her faith and her bravery.

Are we willing to step in when others are afraid to?

[Discover more about Judge Deborah in Judges 4–5.]

Jael

When Barak and the Israelite army rout Sisera's army, Sisera escapes and takes refuge with Jael because her family has a connection with his country. Pretending to protect him, Jael takes him in and cares for him. Once he falls asleep, she impales him with a tent peg through his temple. Though gruesome, it's likely the only means she has to kill him. She is brave enough to act and strong enough to pierce his skull.

This fulfills the prophecy of Judge Deborah who, after Barak's reluctance to obey God, foretells that credit for Sisera's death will go to a woman instead of Barak. As a tribute to her valor, Deborah immortalizes Jael's actions in song.

Will the things we do be worth singing about and told to future generations?

[Discover more about Jael in Judges 4:15–22 and Judges 5:24–27.]

The Mother of Jephthah

Jephthah's father is Gilead. His mother is a prostitute. The Bible doesn't even bother to give her name. So begins the life of Jephthah. When he is older, his half brothers, sons of his father's wife, chase Jephthah away. They don't want him sharing in their inheritance. He leaves, carrying with him the stigma of his bastard birth.

We can only wonder if Jephthah's mother has an ongoing relationship with his dad or if Jephthah's conception is the result of a single night of unrestrained lust. Scripture doesn't say if Jephthah's mother has other children or if she ever pulls herself out of a lifestyle of selling her body.

We don't know if Jephthah's mother is part of his life after he is born or if she retreats with him when he leaves town. Does Jephthah even know who his mom is? Scripture doesn't tell us anything about her life or what forced her into prostitution. We only know that she has a son named Jephthah.

However, we do find out what happens to her son. When the townspeople need help, they know who to turn to. They retrieve Jephthah from exile and elevate him to commander over their army. God's spirit fills Jephthah. He is empowered. Jephthah leads the army into battle and scores a mighty victory, not only for the townspeople but for the entire nation of Israel. Jephthah is a hero, and he leads the people for the rest of his life.

Like Jephthah's mother, we may not be living the life we want. We may not even be able to rise above our situation, but our reality doesn't need to form our children's future. With God's spirit they can rise above their circumstances and succeed. May it be so.

What can we do to help the next generation have a better future?

[Discover more about Jephthah's mom in Judges 11:1–33.]

The Daughter of Jephthah

We don't know the name of Jephthah's daughter. But we lament what happened to her. We applaud the steadfast confidence in how she accepts her fate, revealing her deep faith in God.

The elders of Gilead ask Jephthah to lead them into battle against their enemies. He agrees, but then makes a rash vow. He says that upon his successful return he will give an offering to God. Jephthah pledges to sacrifice the first thing that comes through the door of his house as a burnt offering to thank God for his victory. Jephthah assumes it will be an animal.

He is indeed victorious.

However, to his dismay, the first thing that walks through the door when he returns home is his daughter, his only child. She dances in celebration for his success. He laments the foolish promise he made to God but feels obligated to fulfill it.

Jephthah's daughter doesn't complain about her father's careless pledge. Instead, she confirms he must follow through. Her only request is a two-month reprieve to mourn her fate with her friends. Then Jephthah does as he vowed.

What is unclear is if Jephthah physically sacrifices his daughter, something Moses prohibited, or if her life is redeemed for service to God, like Hannah's giving of Samuel to serve God in the temple. Regardless, it's clear that Jephthah's daughter will not enjoy the future she expected, for she willingly accepts the consequences of her father's impulsive promise to God. We commend her for her pious attitude, all the while being reminded to be careful with what we promise.

When faced with circumstances beyond our control, do we challenge the injustice or accept it with God-honoring dignity?

[Discover more about Jephthah's daughter in Judges 11:30–40.]

The Mother of Samson

There is a woman, the wife of Manoah. She is barren. Though we don't know how long she and Manoah have tried to have children, God sends an angel to her with good news. He promises she will become pregnant and have a boy. However, he also requires something of her.

She must not drink alcohol or eat anything that isn't kosher. Though we might assume this only applies while she is pregnant, the Bible doesn't say that. This might be a lifelong requirement for her, because when she and Manoah later ask the angel how they should raise their baby, the angel repeats these same instructions to her.

As far as their son, he also has restrictions placed on him. He should never cut his hair. They are to raise him as a Nazirite, though Scripture doesn't explain exactly what this means. However, the instructions for living a set-apart life are not just for Samson but also for his mom. If she doesn't do her part, Samson might not be able to do all God has planned for him.

She does indeed get pregnant and gives birth to a baby boy. She names him Samson.

Unfortunately, Samson grows up to have many character flaws, which eventually lead to his downfall. Despite his shortcomings he accomplishes much for God and the nation of Israel. The key to his success, however, may have hinged on his mom's compliance to do what God said. A godly, obedient mother establishes the spiritual framework for Samson to move into his calling and rescue God's people.

Just like Samson's mother, many women change their dietary habits when they are pregnant. They do this to give their baby his or her best chance of enjoying a healthy life. Many moms continue to forgo their personal desires for the sake of their children as they grow up and even after they move into adulthood.

Our sacrifices for others are an expression of our love for them. What are we willing to give up for someone else's benefit?

[Discover more about Samson's mother in Judges 13:2–24.]

Delilah

Though infamous for her tryst with bad-boy Samson, we know little about Delilah. The Bible says Samson falls in love with her. We assume it's mutual, though for her it may just be for the sex or out of rebellion.

Whatever her motivation to hook up with the potent Samson, money soon becomes a more powerful incentive. When the Philistine leaders offer her silver if she can learn the secret behind her lover's strength, she agrees. Eager to earn her reward, she plies Samson to reveal the source of his vigor.

Three times he toys with her, giving misinformation, which she accepts as truth. Each time the Philistines try to use this information to capture him, but they are unable to. Embarrassed over her failures, and no doubt anxious to earn her payoff, she hounds him incessantly. Her nagging eventually wears him down, and he finally breaks. Now knowing the true secret to his strength, the Philistines capture him. Samson later dies in their chains.

Whatever Delilah thinks of Samson at first, she readily sells him out for a few sacks of silver.

What will we do for a paycheck? How far will we go to get money, power, or prestige?

[Discover more about Delilah in Judges 16:4–21.]

Naomi

aomi's name means *pleasant*. Naomi, her husband, and their two boys leave their home country of Judah and travel to Moab because of a famine. While in Moab, Naomi's husband dies, and later both of her married sons die too. This leaves her with two widowed daughters-in-law, Orpah and Ruth, and little hope. Naomi blames God for her misfortune and grows bitter.

She decides to return home when she learns of food there. Orpah and Ruth start back with her, but Naomi decides this isn't fair to them. At Naomi's urging, Orpah returns to Moab and rejoins her family, but Ruth expresses deep commitment to her mother-in-law and to God, promising to stay with her forever and to worship her God.

After returning to Judah, Naomi develops a plan for Ruth to marry their relative, Boaz. Ruth follows her mother-in-law's instructions. Soon Boaz and Ruth marry. Ruth has her first child, Obed. Naomi cares for her new grandson like a son, while the local women celebrate his birth and Naomi's good fortune.

Like all of us, Naomi's life contains struggle and disappointment, but God cares for her, providing a loyal daughter-in-law and a cherished grandson to care for.

Even if life goes terribly wrong and we become bitter and blame God, he still loves us and provides.

Will we trust God with our future, regardless of hardship?

[Discover more about Naomi in Ruth 1–4.]

Ruth

R uth, a widow and foreigner (a non-Hebrew), remains faithful to her widowed mother-in-law, Naomi. When Naomi decides to return home to Judah, she urges Ruth to stay behind in her own country, with her own family. Ruth, however, won't be dissuaded, clinging to her mother-in-law and pledging her allegiance. The reason behind Ruth's intense loyalty to Naomi, however, is a mystery. Having lost her husband and both sons, Naomi is now a bitter woman, so it certainly isn't her personality that causes Ruth's devotion.

When they return to Judah, Ruth, at great personal risk, goes in search of grain missed by the harvesters so she and Naomi will have some food to eat. Ruth finds favor with a wealthy farmer, Boaz, who has heard of her devotion to Naomi and sees her hardworking character.

Naomi wants to find another husband for Ruth. Although much older, Boaz seems the ideal choice. Naomi develops a shrewd strategy for Ruth to capture the heart of Boaz, and Ruth dutifully does as her mother-in-law directs. While it's unclear if Naomi's instructions cause Ruth to act in a manner considered chaste or brazen, she does garner Boaz's attention.

Boaz immediately sets out to make Ruth his wife, deftly dealing with another relative who could thwart his intentions. When Boaz and Ruth marry, the people bless her and her future children.

Ruth has her first child, a boy they name Obed. Obed is the father of Jesse, the father of David. This makes Ruth the great-grandmother of King David.

God rewards Ruth's allegiance to him and loyalty to her mother-in-law, providing Ruth with a husband, saving her from poverty, and giving her a son. Ruth is one of four women honored by Matthew in his record of Jesus's family tree.

Do we have a reputation for being loyal and hardworking? Is our godly character affirmed by others?

[Discover more about Ruth in Ruth 1–4 and Matthew 1:5.]

Orpah

Orpah is the widowed daughter-in-law of Naomi and sister-in-law to Ruth. When Naomi decides to return to Judah, her Moabite daughters-in-law start out with her. Naomi releases them both, encouraging them to return to their mothers and find new husbands. Though Ruth refuses, Orpah does the logical thing and goes home.

That's the last we hear of Orpah. We don't know if she marries again or ever has any children. We don't know how long she lives. We just know she does the sensible thing.

However, Orpah's sister-in-law chooses the path that doesn't make sense, and God honors her for her loyalty to him and her mother-in-law.

Sometimes the sensible solution isn't the one God honors. Do we have the discernment to put God first even if it doesn't make sense?

[Discover more about Orpah in Ruth 1:4–16.]

The Mother of Jabez

Though an entire book was later written about his prayer, we know little about Jabez from Scripture. The Bible only mentions him in two obscure verses, buried in a lengthy genealogy. We know even less about his mother, not even her name.

We do know his birth is difficult, and the name she gives him reflects the physical pain his arrival caused. This is all we know about her.

However, we can infer more of her traits from the character of her son. Jabez is an honorable man, more honorable than others. We also know he has a deep connection with God, for when Jabez prays a bold prayer, God answers it.

We can implicitly connect these qualities with his mother, the woman who raised him. Surely Jabez's mother is a godly woman who teaches her son how to live an honorable life, follow God, and to pray with effectiveness. What more can a mother give to her son?

What can we do to raise godly, honorable, faithful children?

[Discover more about Jabez's mother in 1 Chronicles 4:9–10.]

Hannah

Hannah, married to Elkanah, longs to have children but is childless. To add to her misery, she's harassed by everyone around her. Though she's her husband's favorite wife, he diminishes her infertility. He also fails to protect her from the verbal assaults of his other wife, Peninnah, who endlessly torments her.

Then, when Hannah prays earnestly, Eli, the priest, accuses her of being drunk. But she is actually in deep despair. Her life is in constant turmoil.

At her breaking point, Hannah cries out to God in anguish. She begs him to give her a son. She specifically asks for a boy, not just a child. In return, she promises to give him to God for a lifetime of service.

Unlike everyone else, God understands Hannah. He answers her plea, giving her a son just as she requested. She names him Samuel. Hannah responds by singing her praises to God. She celebrates his power, the elevation of the oppressed, and the judgment of the arrogant.

A few lines of her poem may even be digs at Peninnah, her chief tormentor.

After Samuel is weaned, Hannah presents him to Eli for a lifetime of service to God at the temple, just as she promised. Each year when Hannah and her family make their annual pilgrimage to the temple to offer their sacrifices to God, she sees young Samuel and gives him a new robe. God then blesses Hannah with five more children.

God understands our situation, even when no one else does. Will we trust him to rescue us from our turmoil?

[Discover more about Hannah in 1 Samuel 1–2.]

Peninnah

Peninnah is an unfamiliar Bible character. She is a co-wife with Hannah, the mother of Samuel. Their shared husband is Elkanah.

In a tale reminiscent of Jacob and his two wives, Rachel and Leah, we have the story of Elkanah and his two wives, Hannah and Peninnah. Just as Jacob loves Rachel more than Leah, Elkanah loves Hannah more than Peninnah. Likewise, as Rachel, the favored wife, is childless, so, too, is Hannah.

Another parallel biblical account is of Abraham, Sarah, and Hagar, where Hagar, the wife with a child, harasses Sarah, the wife without one. So too, Peninnah harasses Hannah.

Despite Peninnah producing children for Elkanah, he loves Hannah more. Peninnah lashes out at her rival in the only way possible, by verbally tormenting her each day. While we can't condone Peninnah's actions, we can understand the angst behind them.

When we're in an unbearable situation, do we try to make the best of it or blame others and harass them?

[Discover more about Peninnah in 1 Samuel 1.]

Merab

King Saul has two daughters, Merab and Michal. Merab is the oldest.

Saul offers Merab as a wife for David if he will go to war for Saul, to fight the king's battles for him. But this is a ruse. Saul expects David to die in the military conflict, saving Saul the trouble of killing David himself. Saul never suspects David will return victorious, but when he does, the king reneges on his promise and marries off Merab to another man, Adriel.

Saul never intended for David and Merab to wed. The all-powerful king merely uses her to entice David to do something life-threatening. In this we see a father who exploits his daughter as bait to bring about his enemy's death.

Merab and Adriel have five sons. This is the last we hear about her. The bigger story, however, is not over, for David has eyes for her younger sister, Michal.

Have we ever made a promise we had no intention of keeping?

[Discover more about Merab in 1 Samuel 14:49, 1 Samuel 18:17–21, and 2 Samuel 21:8.]

Michal

David plays a critical role in the success of King Saul and the nation of Israel. Despite this, Saul's attitude toward David varies greatly, with Saul often wanting to kill David out of jealousy. When Saul learns his daughter, Michal, is in love with David, Saul hatches a plan to use her to bring about David's downfall.

For a dowry, Saul requests proof that David has killed one hundred Philistines. Saul assumes David will die trying. Instead, David succeeds, even presenting evidence he's killed twice the requested number.

David and Michal marry.

When Michal learns of her father's plan to kill David, she helps her husband escape and then covers for him. But when her father confronts her duplicity, she lies, claiming David forced her to help.

Some time later, when David is on the run, Saul gives Michal to another man. Eventually, David arranges for Michal's return, and the pair reunite. But they don't live happily ever after. The fact that he has other wives may have something to do with it.

After David ascends to power, he brings the ark back, celebrating wildly in praise to God. Michal criticizes his excessive public display of worship and despises him for his actions. Though she once loved him, she no longer does. We can only guess why. Did his celebratory romp repel her? Perhaps she gave her heart to her second husband, or maybe it was because David married other women.

Regardless, Michal never has any children. Might David have rejected her because of her disapproval of his exuberant dance? Or maybe God punished her for criticizing David's passionate worship. In any regard, a critical spirit is never attractive.

Do we have a critical spirit? What should we do about it?

[Discover more about Michal in 1 Samuel 14:49, 1 Samuel 18–19, 1 Samuel 25:44, 2 Samuel 3:13–14, 2 Samuel 6:16–23, and 1 Chronicles 15:29.]

Abigail (2)

Abigail is an intelligent and beautiful woman. In contrast, her husband, Nabal, is surly and mean. His servants call him wicked and say he listens to no one. Abigail confirms his name means *fool* and that folly follows him. Nabal is also wealthy, with thousands of livestock.

David and his men protect Nabal's herdsmen and flocks, anticipating he will appreciate their efforts and one day reward them. But Nabal disrespects David's messengers when they ask for food, sending them back empty-handed. Roiling with anger, David desires vengeance and prepares to kill Nabal and his men.

When wise Abigail hears what happened, she takes immediate action. She prepares great quantities of food to give to David and goes out to meet his advancing army of four hundred. She humbles herself before David, assumes responsibility (while professing her innocence), wins David over, and stops the massacre.

Abigail then affirms her belief that God will give David a lasting dynasty. She asks him to remember her when God gives him success. David accepts her wise words and her provisions. He blesses her.

But Nabal is incensed when he learns what his wife did, has a stroke, and later dies. David receives this news with glee, seeing it as God's vengeance on his behalf. David sends for Abigail so he can marry her. This may be David fulfilling her request when they first met, or an honorable act to provide for her. However, if their union is for love, Scripture doesn't mention any affection between the pair. For her part, this is the best way to assure survival.

This takes place while David is on the run, so her new lifestyle is not an easy one. At one point, Abigail is captured, along with the rest of the families of David's men, but he rescues her. She and David have one son together, named Daniel.

Abigail takes bold action to avoid a massacre. Is there some bold action God wants us to take?

[Discover more about Abigail in 1 Samuel 25, 1 Samuel 27:2–4, 1 Samuel 30:5, and 1 Chronicles 3:1.]

The Medium of Endor

The prophet Samuel is dead. God has abandoned King Saul, and he is losing his grip on power. Saul prays, but God is silent. None of the ways Saul has heard from God in the past are working now. In desperation, he seeks a medium.

In his better days as God's king, Saul expelled all the mediums and spiritualists from the country. Now he wants one. It's his last option for supernatural guidance. His aids tell him there is a medium in Endor.

In disguise, Saul seeks her out. She is cautious, fearing execution if her skills become known. He persists, promising safety. She relents. Saul asks her to conjure up the spirit of Samuel. She does, and then realizes who Saul is. She screams at him over his deception, but he urges her to proceed.

For Samuel's part, he's not pleased at having his existence in the afterlife disturbed. Samuel confirms it's too late for Saul. God has left him for good. Furthermore,

Samuel says the next day Saul and his sons will die in battle. The nation will be lost.

Saul is distraught, losing what little hope he has left. The medium of Endor urges him to eat, and she prepares a meal for him. Then Saul leaves.

Not all that's spiritual is good. When our prayers seem to go nowhere, do we keep our focus on God or seek ungodly alternatives?

[Discover more about the medium of Endor in 1 Samuel 28:3–25.]

Tamar (2)

The story of Tamar is a tragic one. The beautiful daughter of King David catches the eye of her half brother, Amnon, who lusts for her. At the advice of his cousin, Amnon feigns illness and manipulates Tamar into his bedroom, duping David into innocently arranging the whole thing.

Once alone, Amnon grabs and solicits Tamar. Three times she refuses. When her pleading isn't enough to stop him, she talks about the implications: her disgrace and him appearing as foolish and wicked. In desperation, she even suggests they ask Dad for permission to marry. But Amnon refuses to listen. Lust drives him. He loses control and rapes her.

After this, his supposed love for her turns to an even more intense hate. When he commands her to leave, Tamar refuses, saying that kicking her out would be an even greater insult. Amnon has her forcibly removed from his presence. Tamar, a victim of rape, goes to live in desolation with her brother Absalom.

Is there something we can do to help the victims in our world? Caring for even one person will make a difference.

[Discover more about Tamar in 2 Samuel 13:1–22.]

Bathsheba

Bathsheba, a beautiful woman, is married to Uriah. Despite being a foreigner, Uriah is loyal to the nation of Israel, King David, and God. He is an honorable man, who is off fighting in David's army.

Back home, David, from his palace rooftop vantage, sees Bathsheba bathing. Both are at fault. David shouldn't have been looking, and Bathsheba should have been more discrete. David summons her, so he can sleep with her.

If she does so willingly, that makes her an adulteress and David, an adulterer. If she goes because it's unwise to say "No" to a sovereign king, then David, in effect, rapes her.

Regardless, she becomes pregnant.

To cover up their tryst, David calls Uriah back from the front lines. After two failed attempts to send Uriah home to the arms of his wife, David resorts to plan B. He develops a battle strategy to bring about Uriah's death.

Uriah unwittingly carries that plan with him when he returns to the front lines.

Uriah dies, just as David planned. Bathsheba mourns her husband's death. Then David marries her.

Later, Nathan confronts David for his actions. Once exposed, David acknowledges his mistakes—adultery and murder—and seeks God. However, their love child becomes sick and dies. Later David and Bathsheba have Solomon. Solomon eventually becomes king, just as David promised Bathsheba. Centuries later, Jesus is born. He is David and Bathsheba's direct descendant, through Solomon.

Every pregnancy, whether planned, unplanned, consensual, or forced, carries life and all the potential that life holds.

What can we do to help those with unplanned or un-wanted pregnancies?

[Discover more about Bathsheba in 2 Samuel 11–12, 1 Kings 1:11–31, Psalm 51, and Matthew 1:6.]

The Wise Woman from Tekoa

Joab seeks an object lesson for King David to encourage him to reconcile with his estranged son, Absalom. Joab sends for a wise woman from Tekoa and coaches her what to say to the king.

The story she skillfully shares with the king—of how one son killed the other and is now on the run—is a ruse. Claiming that her surviving son is being sought for murder, she seeks the king's protection. Her pretend story parallels David's real life situation of Absalom killing Amon and then fleeing to another country.

With increasing urgency, three times she asks for David's support. Three times he promises his protection, each time with increased fervency.

Then, with boldness, she connects her story to King David's, asking him to follow his own advice and apply it to his estranged son. David suspects Joab's hand in this and tells Joab to arrange for Absalom's return.

Playing her part brilliantly, the wise woman from Tekoa sets in motion the homecoming of Absalom. Thanks to her, Joab's plan works.

With tact and intelligence, we can influence those in leadership. What should we give our voice to?

[Discover more about the wise woman from Tekoa in 2 Samuel 14:1–20.]

Tamar (3)

Tamar is the daughter of Absalom. She is most beautiful. That's all we know about her. She's likely named after her aunt Tamar, her father's sister who was raped by her uncle Amnon and taken in by her dad, where she lived the rest of her life in desolation.

By sharing her aunt's name, Absalom's daughter Tamar is linked forever to the tragedy that befell her aunt. Like Tamar, our name may be in memory of someone else, which may or may not have positive implications.

However, our name, what it means, or who it's connected to, need not dictate our future. We can shed any implications and pursue our own path.

How can we live our own life, regardless of the labels people give us?

[Discover more about Tamar in 2 Samuel 14:27, along with 2 Samuel 13:1–20.]

Abishag

Abishag is a young, beautiful Shunammite woman, carefully selected to attend to King David in his old age. Despite her sleeping next to him to keep him warm, it isn't sexual.

After David dies, his son Adonijah requests, through Bathsheba, that the new king, King Solomon, allow him to marry Abishag. Though this seems reasonable, Solomon sees this as Adonijah's attempt to elevate his standing in the kingdom and vie for leadership. His apparent power struggle is a threat to Solomon's reign—so Solomon executes Adonijah. We don't know what happens to Abishag.

Abishag has her life in front of her, full of expectations, when she's tapped to be a tool for the king, a human bed warmer. She doesn't even get any "benefits" from the arrangement—though I'm sure people thought otherwise.

When the king dies, it seems her ordeal is over. But it's not. Another man, a wannabe king, tries to use her so he can usurp his half brother's throne. His ploy results in his execution.

Sometimes people use us—or at least they try to. Do we sink to their level or rise above it?

[Discover more about Abishag in 1 Kings 1:1–4 and 1 Kings 2:13–25.]

Two Prostitutes

Two prostitutes share a house. They each get pregnant. First one gives birth, and three days later, the other has a child. Both babies are boys.

One night the unthinkable happens. In her sleep, the second woman rolls on top of her son and he dies. When she realizes what she did, she switches babies and goes back to bed as though nothing happened.

When the first woman goes to nurse her son, she finds he is dead, but in the morning light she realizes it isn't her baby. Her son is in the arms of the other woman. But the second woman claims it's all a lie, that the living son is, in fact, hers.

The pair comes before King Solomon, seeking his intervention. Each one claims the living baby is hers, and insists the dead child belongs to the other woman. They argue with each other in front of the king.

Solomon says the solution is simple. Cut the living baby in two and give half to each woman.

The second woman, the one who is lying, says this is fine. She reasons that this way neither of them will have him. But the first woman, the true mom, shows her love for her boy. She says not to cut him in half, to give the boy to the other woman. She wants him to live, even if it means having another woman raise him.

Solomon realizes the first woman is the true mother and gives her the child. His ruse works, allowing him to discern the truth.

Are we willing to give up the people we love the most if it's in their best interest?

[Discover more about these two women in 1 Kings 3:16–28.]

The Queen of Sheba

The queen of Sheba hears about the stunning reputation of King Solomon. Skeptical, she travels to meet him to see if there is any truth to the reports she has heard. Bringing gifts, she talks with Solomon at length and is astounded with what she sees. The king answers her every question, able to fully explain all things to her.

She then affirms his great wisdom and immense wealth, declaring that what she heard failed to communicate the fullness of all she saw and experienced. She is in awe.

Solomon loads her up with gifts, and she returns home.

The queen of Sheba had to see to believe. Does our confidence in God require tangible proof, or do we have the faith to believe without seeing?

[Discover more about the queen of Sheba in 1 Kings 10:1–13 and 2 Chronicles 9:1–12. See "The Queen of the South" for part 2 of this story, but we won't encounter it until we get to the New Testament.]

The Shulammite Woman

The Song of Solomon records the delightful dalliance of two lovers, madly passionate for one another. They long to be together, inhaling each other's scent, enjoying each other's embrace, cuddling—and more—in each other's bed. Nothing and no one will keep them apart.

Their account, reminiscent of a screenplay, records only dialogue. It features the beloved, played by a captivating, but unnamed, Shulammite woman, and her lover, played by King Solomon. Though noted for his many wives and concubines, none compares to the alluring lass from Shulam.

A careful reading of the story uncovers some provocative, poetic euphemisms for the sexual intimacy the two lovers desire. Some portions border on high-class erotica. Yet the Bible includes these passages for us to read.

How has society skewed our understanding of passion? What is God's plan for sex and pleasure? Do we need to change our perspective?

[Discover more about the woman from Shulam in Song of Songs.]

The Woman of Proverbs 31

The book of Proverbs ends with a poem about a woman of noble character. Though she may be a real person, this passage reads more like an idealized ode to a wife of mythical proportions.

Regardless, she is one busy lady, and I get tired just reading about all she does. She cares for her husband and provides for her family, she works hard with her hands and stays up late, she is an entrepreneur who turns a profit, and she even has time to help the poor. Because of her, her husband enjoys respect.

Her children bless her, and her husband praises her. She's esteemed for her character, dignity, strength, and wisdom. She receives honor and praise. Besides all this, she's beautiful and charming, but she doesn't concern herself with these temporary traits.

Instead, she focuses on something lasting: her relationship with God. She reverences him, having a holy respect for who he is. Today we might understand this as a genuine love for God. Despite being busier than

I can imagine, she still has time for her Lord. Think about it.

While many people look in disbelief at what this woman does, they miss the main point. Our focus should be on who she is: a godly woman who makes God a priority.

Do we give God first place in our lives?

[Discover more about this remarkable woman in Proverbs 31:10–31.]

The Wives of Solomon

Solomon, the wisest man who ever lived, isn't so smart when it comes to his love life. In all, he amasses seven hundred wives and three hundred concubines. Even worse, many of his wives are foreigners, something God prohibits because he fears they will distract his people from fully worshiping him. Unfortunately, just as God predicted, Solomon's foreign-born wives lead him astray and cause him to turn from God later in his life.

These women have no say in their marriage to the king or in being used as a means for his sexual gratification. They represent a political alliance or serve as a means for wanton indulgence, not love in a committed relationship.

For some women the same is true today, and we must fight for their rights. Others have a say in who they marry. They should choose wisely.

Are we willing to trust God with our life partner?

[Discover more about Solomon's many wives in Exodus 34:16, 1 Kings 4:29–31, and 1 Kings 11:1–13.]

Jezebel (1)

Ahab, perhaps Israel's evilest king ever, marries Jezebel, daughter of a foreign ruler. Under her depraved influence, Ahab starts worshiping her gods, instead of the true God. Jezebel hunts down and kills God's prophets, while she provides sanctuary for hundreds of the prophets of Baal and Asherah.

God's prophet Elijah has a public smackdown with the prophets of Baal and Asherah that results in him killing them all. In retaliation, Jezebel threatens to likewise kill Elijah. While he's on the run, Jezebel adds to her crimes by orchestrating an innocent man's death to seize his vineyard for her husband.

Eventually, Jezebel suffers a gruesome death, just as prophesied.

Though evil people sometimes seem to suffer no consequences for their foul behavior, God's judgment ultimately prevails.

How do we react when confronted with evil?

[Discover more about Jezebel in 1 Kings 16:31, 1 Kings 18:4–19, 1 Kings 19:1–2, 1 Kings 21:5–24, and 2 Kings 9:7–37.]

The Widow of Zarephath

During a long drought and famine, God sends Elijah away from Israel to the foreign city of Zarephath in Sidon. When Elijah reaches the town gates, he sees a woman, a widow, and asks her for water and bread. Though she is willing to fetch him water, she has no bread to share. In fact, she plans to use her last remaining bit of oil and flour to make a final meal for herself and her son before they starve to death.

Elijah tells her not to worry, to go home and prepare this meal for herself and her boy—but to first make a small loaf of bread for him. He tells her that her flour and oil will last until it rains again. She does as he asks. As promised, the flour and oil last, providing food for the three of them every day.

After a while, her son dies. The woman blames Elijah. He takes the dead boy to his room, imploring God to restore life to the lad. God does as Elijah asks. When Elijah presents the resurrected boy to the widow, she finally realizes Elijah is a man of God.

Centuries later, Jesus recounts this story, reminding the people that God didn't send Elijah to any of the needy widows in Israel but to a foreigner. This infuriates them, and they try to kill Jesus, but he walks through the mob and leaves.

Sometimes God asks us to do things that seem ill-advised. The widow of Zarephath did what was illogical and lived.

Are we willing to do what God says even if it doesn't make sense?

[Discover more about the widow of Zarephath in 1 Kings 17:7–24 and Luke 4:24–26.]

The Widow and Her Oil

The widow of one of Elisha's followers comes to him for help. Her deceased husband left her with an outstanding debt. She has no means to pay off his loan, and the creditor demands her two sons become his slaves as payment.

Elisha asks what resources she has. "Nothing," she replies. "Just a small amount of olive oil."

Elisha has a plan. He tells her to borrow empty jars from her neighbors, lots of them. Then she is to go home, close the doors, and begin pouring olive oil from her small vessel into all the other jars. She does, and the oil continues to flow until every container is full. When she has no more to fill, the oil stops flowing.

She sells the oil. With the proceeds, she pays off her debt and has extra to live on.

What if she had borrowed more jars? What if she had only borrowed a few?

When God tells us to do something, do we do it halfway and possibly miss his bounty, or do we go all out?

[Discover more about the poor widow and her oil in 2 Kings 4:1–7.]

The Shunammite Woman

Elisha travels to the city of Shunem, and a wealthy woman urges him to stay for a meal. From then on, whenever he's in the area, he stops by. Realizing he's a man of God, she makes a room for him to stay in when he's in town.

Grateful, Elisha wants to do something nice for her. She has no son. And with an aging husband, they have no expectation of ever having kids. Elisha prophesies that within a year, she will have a boy.

As promised, a year later she gives birth to a son.

When the boy grows older, one day his head begins to hurt, and he dies in her arms. She puts him in Elisha's room. Without telling her husband what happened, she searches for the prophet. With great intent, she finds him, but then blames him for raising her hopes in the first place, when she didn't even ask for a son.

The prophet sends his servant to resurrect the boy, but she refuses to leave Elisha. So the two of them head for her home. It's a good thing they do, because despite

PETER DEHAAN, PHD

following what Elisha instructed, his servant can't resurrect the boy. Though it takes a couple of tries, Elisha
brings the boy back to life.

Later, Elisha warns the woman of a seven-year famine and sends her away to another country. When she
returns, the king restores her land to her, along with the
profits it generated while she was gone.

The Shunammite woman honored God by caring
for his prophet. As a result, God cared for her, through
both good times and bad.

What can we do to honor God?

[Discover more about the woman from Shunem in 2
Kings 4:8–37 and 2 Kings 8:1–6.]

The Servant of Naaman

An unnamed Israelite girl is captured in a raid and forced to work as a slave in the household of the enemy commander, Naaman. Although Naaman is an accomplished military leader, he suffers from a limiting physical ailment. He has leprosy, a contagious skin disease that can cause a loss of feeling, flesh decay, and even deformation.

Though she could have been bitter over her forced servitude, the young girl instead desires the best for her master. She tells him of the prophet Elisha, who can heal Naaman of his terrible disease. Naaman proceeds at once and receives God's healing—as soon as he humbles himself and follows Elisha's instructions.

Naaman then affirms the power of God and pledges to worship only him.

Though she has every reason to remain quiet, the girl's confidence in God's power and her willingness to speak up leads to a man receiving healing and God receiving praise.

How willing are we to help others, regardless of our situation?

[Discover more about Naaman's servant girl in 2 Kings 5:1–19.]

Two Starving Women

In perhaps the most gut-wrenching story in the Bible, two women conspire to do the unthinkable. The city of Samaria is under siege. Supplies are scarce and food is running out. To survive, the people resort to eating whatever they can find, such as the head of a donkey or dove droppings.

In their deep hunger, two women agree to a most depraved scheme: to eat their children. They cook and eat one woman's son, but when it comes time to eat the other boy, his mom hides him. The first woman appeals to the king for justice. He can do nothing but lament their barbarism.

If only the women had waited. The next day the siege ends when the enemy abandons their blockade in a panic, leaving all their supplies behind. There is plenty of food for everyone.

How often do we grow tired of waiting for God and do something rash?

[Discover more about these two women in 2 Kings 6:24–31 and 2 Kings 7:1–16.]

Athaliah

Athaliah is an evil woman. She encourages her son, the king, to make some ill-advised decisions. He does and is soon assassinated. Then Athaliah seizes control and asserts herself as queen. Her lust for power is so great that she kills all the members of the royal family, including her own grandchildren.

One baby, however, is rescued by his aunt, Jehosheba. His name is Joash. Six years later, he, the rightful heir to the throne, is crowned king by the priest with the support of the Levites and heads of the leading families.

Athaliah accuses them of treason and tears her clothes to express outrage. But she can't change what happened. At the direction of the priest, the army kills her.

The country celebrates her death and calm returns.

Athaliah could have positively influenced her son and helped him rule wisely. She could have protected and groomed his successor. Had she done so, the people might have celebrated her life. Instead, they celebrated her death.

How do we want people to remember us?

[Discover more about Athaliah in 2 Kings 11 and 2 Chronicles 22–23.]

Jehosheba

At great personal risk, probably execution, Jehosheba takes bold action to keep her nephew Joash from being killed by his evil grandmother, who has seized power and is wiping out the royal family. Jehosheba likely has little time to consider her actions when she rescues Joash from among the royal princes who are about to be killed.

Jehosheba hides Joash and his nurse in the temple for six years. When Joash is seven, he's crowned king and his power-hungry grandmother is slain. The people rejoice and peace returns, all because of the boy-king and his aunt who made it possible.

Jehosheba plays a decisive role in protecting the rightful heir to the throne, keeping him alive so that he could one day rule and restore peace to the land.

Sometimes we must react quickly, with little time to analyze the situation. May we all be like Jehosheba, who acted decisively to do the right thing without concern for her own wellbeing.

What do we need to do regardless of the personal risk?

[Discover more about Jehosheba in 2 Kings 11:2 and 2 Chronicles 22:11.]

Gomer

Gomer is a prostitute, likely working the temple of Baal. She uses her only marketable skill to put food in her stomach and clothes on her back. She is certainly not marriage material, especially not for a man of God. Yet, in a shocking move, God tells his young prophet Hosea to marry a prostitute.

Hosea picks Gomer. They marry, but they don't have a happy union.

They have a son together. Then she has two more children, but Hosea doubts he's their father. The first, a girl, Hosea names Lo-Ruhamah, which means *no pity* or *not loved*. The second, a boy, he names Lo-Ammi, which means *not mine*.

God then prompts Hosea to use his relationship with Gomer and her illegitimate kids as sermon illustrations in his scathing rebuke against the nations of Israel and Judah for their unfaithfulness to God.

Then Gomer runs off and takes up with another lover. At God's direction, Hosea goes after her. He must buy her freedom. He tells her to stop running around, to be faithful to him. He offers her undeserved love and even accepts her two kids who another man fathered.

Hosea married Gomer even though she was undeserving. And he offered her unconditional love when she ran away.

So it is with God and us.

How far are we willing to go to show love to others when they hurt us badly?

[Discover more about Gomer in Hosea 1–3 and Hosea 14:4.]

Lo-Ruhamah

L o-Ruhamah is the daughter of Gomer, the product of an affair. Her mom, a former prostitute, cheats on her husband and hooks up with someone more appealing. Understandably, the child's stepdad, Hosea, rejects his wife's daughter. To make sure everyone knows he's not the dad, he names her Lo-Ruhamah, which means *no pity* or *not loved*.

What a terrible way to begin life. What a condemning legacy to carry. Each time someone calls her name, it serves as a painful reminder to Lo-Ruhamah of being rejected by the only man in her life.

Eventually Hosea reconciles with his wife. He accepts Lo-Ruhamah as his daughter and loves her. We wonder how Lo-Ruhamah responds. Does she rise above the conditions of her birth or does she remain forever wounded?

Though all parents fall short in childrearing, that's not an excuse for not making the best of our lives. We don't get to choose our parents, but we can choose how we respond to their mistakes in raising us.

How can we best react to the situation we find ourselves in?

[Discover more about Lo-Ruhamah in Hosea 1:6 and Hosea 2:23.]

Noadiah

Noadiah is a prophetess during the time of Nehemiah when he leads the people in rebuilding the wall in Jerusalem. There is opposition to Nehemiah and his mission from some of the local people. They merely seem to want to stir up trouble.

His chief opponents are Tobiah and Sanballat. They also enlist the help of a few others, including Geshem and Shemaiah. Tobiah and Sanballat pay Shemaiah to give Nehemiah bad advice, but Nehemiah discerns Shemaiah's duplicity, accusing Shemaiah of prophesying against him.

Immediately after this, Nehemiah turns his detractors over to God for punishment. He lists Tobiah and Sanballat by name, but not Geshem and Shemaiah. He does, however, mention another person, the prophetess Noadiah. He says she and the rest of the prophets tried to intimidate him.

While several chapters in the Bible detail the efforts of Tobiah and Sanballat to derail Nehemiah's mission, this is the first we hear about Noadiah, her efforts to intimidate, and her misguided influence over the other prophets. We don't know the details of what she did or why Nehemiah was so vexed with her, but we do know that after Tobiah and Sanballat, Nehemiah views her as his third biggest nemesis.

Noadiah could have used her status as prophetess for good or for bad. She chose wrong.

How can we best use our position, skills, and abilities to support God's purpose and not oppose him?

[Discover more about Noadiah in Nehemiah 6:14.]

Queen Vashti

Queen Vashti, wife of the mighty Persian King Xerxes, gives a weeklong party for the women in the palace. At the same time, her husband throws his own celebration, complete with an open bar.

On day seven, an intoxicated Xerxes commands the beautiful Vashti to parade herself before his drunken guests. When the chaste Vashti refuses to debase herself and be subjected to their ogling eyes, the king is furious.

Embarrassed, the enraged ruler asks his advisors what to do. Their answer is unequivocal: depose Vashti and forever bar her from his presence. The king does as they suggest, issuing an irrevocable edict.

Though Queen Vashti acts with virtue and refuses to stoop to the king's drunken depravity, she pays a heavy price for maintaining her integrity. Sometimes there are consequences for doing what is right. May we hold to our principles and persevere despite the outcome.

How much value do we place on our integrity? How much will we risk to do what's right?

[Discover more about Queen Vashti in Esther 1:7–20.]

Queen Esther

After King Xerxes banishes Queen Vashti from his presence, he regrets his irrevocable edict. His aides suggest a plan to find a replacement. Their proposal is to round up the most beautiful virgins in the land for the king to try out. Yes, it is as bad as it sounds.

The most pleasing one will be crowned queen. This isn't a voluntary beauty pageant. This is conscripted service that forces the selected women into a harem. They effectively become well-cared-for sex slaves. Esther (Hadassah) is rounded up in their dragnet. She waits at least four years for her assigned time to sleep with the king.

Finally, it's her turn. Though inexperienced, Esther's night with the king must have been most pleasing to him, because the next morning, he proclaims her queen. This, however, is not a Cinderella story where she lives happily ever after.

In the expanded version of this story, found in some Bibles, Esther says she abhors sleeping with the king. As an uncircumcised foreigner, he repulses her. She finds no joy in her position as queen. However, aside from involuntary sex with the king, she keeps herself true to her upbringing.

Later, when Haman plots the Jews' extermination, Esther is challenged by Mordecai, her cousin who adopted her, to intervene with the king on the Jews' behalf. She balks. It's been a month since she's seen the king and she risks immediate execution by appearing before him without being summoned. Mordecai begs Esther to take the risk, saying, "What if God put you in this position so you could address this situation?"

Eventually she agrees: "If I die, then I die." In preparation, Esther fasts for three days and asks others to fast with her.

When she approaches the king, he spares her life. However, instead of directly appealing to him, she invites him and Haman to a private banquet with her. She then requests they come a second evening and at that time she reveals Haman's plot, appealing to the king for justice. Because of her actions, Haman is executed, and the Jews are spared. The Purim celebrates Esther and her heroics in saving the people.

Though she needed to think about it and took time to fast, Esther bravely set her own safety aside and risked her life to save others.

Are we willing to save lives regardless of the risk?

[Discover more about Queen Esther in Esther 2:7–17, 4:1–17, 5:1–7, 7:1–10, and 9:12–15. For more information, see "Bonus Material: The Full Picture."]

Zeresh

Zeresh is the wife of the anti-Semitic Haman.

Enraged that Mordecai, a Jew, slighted him, Haman plots the annihilation of all Jewish people scattered throughout the Persian Empire. Later, when complaining about Mordecai to his family and friends, Zeresh recommends he erect a seventy-five-foot pole and seek the king's permission to impale Mordecai on it. Haman delights in this suggestion and follows his wife's advice.

His plan is foiled, however, when the king has a different idea. Instead of executing his nemesis, the king commands Haman to honor Mordecai. Completing this distasteful task, the mortified Haman returns home in humiliation. Then Zeresh predicts Haman's downfall. Since Mordecai is a Jew, she says, Haman doesn't stand a chance.

She's correct.

A few days later Haman is impaled on the same pole he constructed for Mordecai's execution. Zeresh's initial advice to her husband becomes the tool for his death. Zeresh gave her husband the guidance he wanted to hear. What if she had counseled him differently, instead encouraging him to rise above his vendetta and not seek revenge?

When we give advice to others, do we offer them the easy answer or the right one?

[Discover more about Zeresh in Esther 5:9–14 and Esther 6:12–14.]

Foreign Women

Throughout the history of the nation of Israel and Judah, a recurring theme is Hebrew men marrying foreign women. This is something God forbids. It isn't that God hates other ethnicities. They are part of his creation too.

Instead, he gives his people this restriction because he knows if the men involve themselves with women who hold other beliefs, the men's attention will turn from him to other gods and from holy practices to unholy behaviors. God wants his people to worship him only, to do so with purity and purpose. He desires them to raise their children to do the same.

Throughout the Old Testament, when the men stray from God's command and give their physical affections to women of other faiths, they also end up giving their spiritual attention to other gods. Disaster results.

Later Paul commands the people in the Corinthian church to not yoke themselves with unbelievers. In explaining such a pairing, he uses two contrasting sets of words: righteousness and wickedness, light and darkness. While this instruction to not be unequally paired with others can apply to close friendships and business partnerships, the most critical application is marriage.

Starting in the Old Testament and continuing into the New Testament, we're encouraged to marry people who share our faith. Failing to do so will only cause problems.

This is a great lesson for those not yet married and a comfort to those married to someone who shares their essential beliefs, but what about those who are married to an unbeliever?

To those already in marriages with unbelievers, Paul offers some practical advice. He says if the unbelieving spouse is willing to stay in the marriage, do not seek divorce. The nonbelieving partner will receive blessings through his or her spouse and their children are likewise set apart for God. In time, the unbelieving spouse may one day believe in God, but this is not a guarantee, just a possibility. However, if the unbelieving spouse wants to leave, Paul allows it.

The main principle is to seek to live in peace. Paul ends his teaching by saying we should remain faithful to our beliefs whatever our situation.

Whether in marriage, business, or key friendships, we should seek godly partners in all situations. And if we are unequally yoked, we should hold to our faith and be an example, pointing others to Jesus.

In what ways might we be unequally yoked? How have we allowed others to distract us from God?

[Discover more about foreign women in Exodus 34:11–16, Deuteronomy 7:1–4, 1 Kings 11:1, Ezra 9:2, Ezra 10:2–44, Nehemiah 13:26–27, Malachi 2:11, 1 Corinthians 7:12–17, and 2 Corinthians 6:14.]

Susanna (1)

*S*usanna and the four women who follow aren't in all versions of the Bible. Their stories, however, are in The New Jerusalem Bible, Common English Bible (CEB), and New American Bible (NAB). They also appeared in the original translation of the King James Version (KJV). For more information, see "Bonus Material: The Full Picture."

Susanna lives in exile in Babylon. She is known for her great beauty and deep reverence for God. Her parents are moral folks, conducting themselves with virtue, which they instill in their daughter. Susanna's husband is rich and respected by the people. The leading Jews hang out at his house. Aside from being displaced from her homeland, Susanna enjoys an idyllic life.

However, two of the elders, appointed as judges, are obsessed with Susanna. They lust for her. This is consistent with their corrupt behavior as immoral judges. They could have looked away, but they choose not to.

Conspiring to rape her, they hide in her private garden and ogle her. When she is alone, they reveal themselves and solicit her. If she refuses, they threaten to tell everyone they caught her cheating on her husband with another man. The penalty for adultery is death.

Trapped in a no-win situation, Susanna decides to act morally. She turns them down and screams for help.

When people come running, the judges lie, "We caught her having sex with this guy. We tried to stop him, but he got away." Because of their position, everyone believes them and sentences Susanna to death.

No one asks for her side of the story.

As they haul her off for execution, the Holy Spirit reveals the truth to the young prophet Daniel. He yells out that she's innocent. Separating the two men, Daniel cross-examines them and they contradict each other, proving they gave false testimony against Susanna. The perverted men are convicted, and the righteous Susanna is freed, with her reputation restored.

Susanna faced a terrible choice: have sex with two men and live or be wrongly convicted of adultery and die. It may have seemed best to give in, but Susanna did the right thing and trusted God to vindicate her. He came through.

How willing are we to do what's right despite the risk?

[Discover more about Susanna in Daniel 13 in The New Jerusalem Bible and NAB (also known as the book of Susanna in the CEB). For more information, see "Bonus Material: The Full Picture."]

Deborah (3)

D eborah is the grandmother of Tobit. She raises him after his parents die. She teaches him about their faith, training him in the regulations Moses received from God and taught to the people.

She also instills in him a deep generosity. Not only does he give what is required to the temple, priests, and Levites, but at her encouragement, he also gives 10 percent of his income to poor people in Jerusalem and another 10 percent to orphans, widows, and converts to Judaism.

Thanks to his grandma's influence, Tobit has a heart to help others. While most grandparents don't have to raise their grandkids, most every grandparent can influence them.

How can we be sure to make the most of our opportunities to inspire others?

[Discover more about Deborah in Tobit 1:6–8 in The New Jerusalem Bible, Common English Bible (CEB), and New American Bible (NAB). For more information, see "Bonus Material: The Full Picture."]

Sarah (2)

S arah is sensible, brave, and beautiful. She's been married seven times and is also seven times a widow, for each time on her wedding night, a demon kills her new husband. When falsely accused of murdering all seven, she plans to commit suicide. However, wishing to spare her father the grief, she doesn't. Instead she prays, giving God the option to take her life if he is displeased with her conduct.

God hears her prayer but has another solution in mind. He sets in motion the events to rescue her.

Meanwhile, Tobias embarks on a quest of epic scope. At the prompting of an angel, he stops by to ask Sarah's father for permission to marry her. Though he's never met her, he's her closest living relative and next in line to marry her, according to Jewish custom. When Tobias finally meets her, it's love at first sight. Despite the risk of the demon killing him on their wedding night too, Tobias still wants her. Sarah's father agrees. They sign the wedding contract.

That night Tobias mixes a potion and burns it. The smell chases away the demon. Then Tobias and Sarah ask God to protect them through the night. He does. For the first time in eight tries, Sarah's husband is still alive at daybreak.

Sarah's family then celebrates for two weeks before the happy couple leaves. When they reach Tobias's home, there's a grand reunion and another weeklong wedding celebration.

Sarah's life was a mess and her future, bleak. No one could fault her for giving up. But instead of suicide, she sought God. He rescued her, removing the curse and protecting her new husband.

When life overwhelms us, do we quit or seek God?

[Discover more about Sarah in Tobit 3:7–16, Tobit 6:10–18, Tobit 7:9–16, Tobit 8:1–21, Tobit 10:10–13, and Tobit 11:15–18 in The New Jerusalem Bible, Common English Bible (CEB), and New American Bible (NAB). For more information, see "Bonus Material: The Full Picture."]

Judith (2)

Judith (2) is a widow whose wealthy husband left her well provided for. Though quite beautiful, she hides her good looks under the garb of mourning. A righteous woman, she fasts regularly and conducts herself beyond reproach. All people esteem her.

With Judith's city, Bethulia, under siege, food is scarce, and water is rationed. The mayor promises to surrender in five days, hoping God will miraculously save them by then. But Judith chastises him for his willingness to give up. She has a plan, a bold strategy, to save them, but she won't tell anyone what it is.

She cleans up and replaces her widow's clothing with festive attire, complete with perfume, jewelry, and a tiara. It's her most alluring look. The people can't believe the transformation. Then she and her maid leave the city and allow themselves to be captured.

Promising to aid the enemy, Judith is taken to their commander, Holofernes. Weaving partial truth into her ruse, Judith unveils her proposal of how she will advise him in taking the city without any loss of life. Enthralled by her beauty, Holofernes believes every word she says. Besides, he also wants to sleep with her.

After a couple of days and willing to wait no longer, he summons her to join him in his tent for dinner. They eat, and he drinks—too much. He sends everyone away so he can seduce her. But he passes out instead, with Judith's virtue still intact. Judith grabs his sword, prays for supernatural strength, and decapitates him with two blows.

Judith and her maid sneak off before anyone knows what happened, carrying his severed head with them. Arriving home, the people celebrate as she tells them what happened and holds up the proof.

When the soldiers find the body of their headless leader, they're thrown into a panic and flee. The Jews in Bethulia summon their countrymen throughout Israel to give chase, slaughtering their enemy and enjoying the spoils. The people celebrate Judith for her heroic exploit.

Taking much risk, Judith daringly delivers her people from their enemies, using her beauty to entice, while remaining pure.

Great results often require great risk. How much are we willing to risk to do what God calls us to do?

[Discover more about Judith in Judith 8–16 in The New Jerusalem Bible, Common English Bible (CEB), and New American Bible (NAB). For more information, see "Bonus Material: The Full Picture."]

The Maid of Judith

The story of Judith's bravery is inspiring. Although it is Judith who perfectly executes her daring plan, she does not go alone. Her maid accompanies her, taking as much risk as Judith. Consider the role of Judith's maid.

First, she summons the town's officials, demanding they come talk to Judith. Next, she goes with Judith to the enemy, allowing themselves to be captured and taken into the heart of the enemy camp. Then she stands watch outside the tent while Judith kills Holofernes inside. Last, she carries his severed head as they make their escape in the middle of the night.

Though Judith's maid did not volunteer for this assignment, she does everything she's told to do. Without her help, the outcome of Judith's mission would be in doubt.

After their safe return, the trouncing of their enemy, gathering up the spoils, and the lengthy celebration that follows, Judith rewards her maid by granting her freedom.

Sometimes we have little choice in the things we must do, but we do have a choice in how well we do them. Judith's maid acquits herself well and receives a reward for her bravery and her actions.

When tasked with an unpleasant or even risky undertaking, do we try to get out of it, or do we do our best to succeed?

[Discover more about Judith's maid in Judith 8:10, Judith 10:10–12, Judith 13:2, 9, and Judith 16:23 in The New Jerusalem Bible, Common English Bible (CEB), and New American Bible (NAB). For more information, see "Bonus Material: The Full Picture."]

WOMEN IN THE NEW TESTAMENT

Elizabeth

Childless, Elizabeth and her husband, Zechariah, are getting old. Their chance to have kids is slim. Still, they pray for the improbable. Despite not receiving what they yearn for, their faith remains strong. They're a righteous couple who honor God.

One day at work, an angel shows up and promises Zechariah that he and Elizabeth will finally have a son—not just any son but a special one. He is to be set apart for service to God, the Holy Spirit will empower him, and he will spark a nationwide revival.

They are to name him John.

Elizabeth does indeed get pregnant. In her sixth month, Mary—who is also expecting—comes for a visit. Inside Elizabeth, baby John jumps for joy at the sound of Mary's voice. Then the Holy Spirit comes upon Elizabeth and she prophesies, blessing Mary and her unborn child.

When John is born, Elizabeth and Zechariah's friends and family celebrate with them. They praise God and share in Elizabeth's joy for finally having a baby.

Elizabeth and Zechariah prayed for a child even when it no longer made sense. God answered their prayers by giving them a son named John. We call him John the Baptist.

Are we willing to pray for the impossible? Will we patiently wait for God's answer?

[Discover more about Elizabeth in Luke 1:5–60.]

Mary (1)

An angel visits Mary, a young girl engaged to be married. The angel celebrates her as one highly favored by God. Perplexed, Mary wonders about the angel's shocking greeting. Then he further stuns her by saying she will become pregnant, and her child will save her people.

"How?" Mary asks. "I'm a virgin."

The angel explains that the Holy Spirit will supernaturally impregnate her.

Mary trusts God in this and accepts the angel's words without arguing.

When Joseph, her fiancé, finds out she's with child, he plans to end their engagement, but an angel visits him, too, and tells him not to break up with her. They get married, but they remain celibate until after Mary's miracle baby is born.

However, before this happens Mary and Joseph must travel to Bethlehem for a mandatory census. Unable to find a place to stay, they hunker down in a barn. There, among the filth of livestock, Jesus is born.

This is no ordinary birth. Angels celebrate, shepherds bow down, and royalty offer expensive gifts. Then at Jesus's consecration, people give astounding prophecies and thanks for him. Twelve years later, Jesus amazes his parents, especially Mary, when they find him at the temple in deep discussion with the religious leaders.

At age thirty he starts his ministry. Three years later, during his execution, Jesus makes sure Mary will be cared for. The last we hear of her is at a gathering of Jesus's followers after he rises from the dead and returns to heaven.

Though we praise Mary for her pious acceptance of God's assignment, the townspeople didn't likely celebrate her circumstances. They certainly dismissed her claim that "God did it," and she likely forever carried the stigma of the girl who got pregnant before she was married.

Sometimes there is a price for following God. Would we be willing to suffer a lifetime of humiliation to conform to his plan for us?

[Discover more about Mary in Matthew 1:18–2:11, Luke 1:26–38, Luke 2:1–51, and Acts 1:14.]

Anna (2)

Anna is widowed after only seven years of marriage. A devout woman, she dedicates her life to God, spending as much time as possible in the temple, fasting, praying, and worshiping him.

She is at least eighty-four years old when Mary and Joseph show up to consecrate Jesus. She recognizes him as the savior the people have been expecting for centuries. She thanks God she has lived long enough to see Jesus and then shares her excitement with everyone nearby.

After a lifetime of devotion to God, Anna receives her reward by seeing Jesus. How many other people were likewise as devout, but never got to meet baby Jesus?

God calls us to focus on him, but we may not receive any reward for our loyalty during our lifetime. Will we be faithful anyway?

[Discover more about Anna in Luke 2:36–38.]

Herodias

Herod is a powerful man, used to getting what he wants. He even takes his brother's wife, Herodias, and marries her. John the Baptist publicly criticizes Herod for his actions, stating plainly that what he did is illegal, contrary to the Laws of Moses. For his boldness, John ends up in jail. Herod holds him there, keeping him out of public view, while at the same time protecting him from further harm.

We don't know if Herodias is the victim in this adulterous marriage or the instigator, but the Bible says she holds a grudge against John for his criticism. In fact, she's so enraged, she wants him dead, but Herod won't allow it. He knows John is a good man, and Herod likes to listen to him—even though John's words perplex him.

When Herod throws a birthday party for himself, Herodias's daughter dances for them. Everyone likes what they see. Because of her impressive performance,

Herod, without thinking, promises to give her whatever she wants. She seeks her mom's advice.

Herodias sees opportunity and is quick to respond. She tells her daughter to ask for John's head on a platter.

Although dismayed, Herod doesn't want to renege on his promise in front of his guests. To avoid public embarrassment, he orders John's immediate execution. They present John's head on a platter to the girl.

Blinded by anger, Herodias achieves her goal of orchestrating John's death. She gets her revenge.

While we would never plot another person's death, Jesus says even anger toward another is akin to murder. What raw emotions do we need to curb?

[Discover more about Herodias in Matthew 14:3–14, Mark 6:17–28, and Luke 3:19–20.]

The Daughter of Herodias

The daughter of Herodias dances for her stepdad at his birthday party. We don't know if she offers her performance or if Herod commands it. And we don't know what kind of dance this is. Is it an innocent expression of joy or a suggestive display of sexuality? What we do know is that her performance pleases everyone. So enamored, her stepdad promises her anything she wants.

Unsure of what to ask for, she seeks her mom's advice, who coaches her on what to request: the head of John the Baptist. The daughter does what her Mom says, and Herod reluctantly follows through.

Herodias uses her daughter—who is innocent of wrongdoing—to bring about the death of her enemy.

Has someone ever used us to accomplish their selfish goals? What could we have done to avoid it?

[Discover more about Herodias's daughter in Matthew 14:6–14 and Mark 6:21–28.]

The Mother-In-Law of Peter

I don't think of any of Jesus's twelve disciples as being married, but we know that at least Peter is—because we learn he has a mother-in-law. We see her only once in the Bible, and she's not at her best. She's incapacitated by a severe fever.

When Jesus comes to Peter's house, he sees Peter's ailing mother-in-law, touches her hand, and the fever goes away. To show her appreciation, she gets up and serves Jesus, making a meal for him.

Jesus has done much more for us than taking away a fever. What are we doing to show our gratitude?

[Discover more about Peter's mother-in-law in Matthew 8:14–15.]

The Widow from Nain

A woman from the town of Nain has sorrow heaped upon sorrow. First her husband dies. Then her only son perishes. At that time, the culture dismisses a woman without a male in her family, such as a husband or son.

This woman's future is indeed bleak.

During the funeral procession for her boy, a large crowd follows along, mourning with her and sharing in her grief. Jesus comes up to the group, and his heart goes out to the woman. He touches the coffin. The pallbearers stop. Jesus speaks to the dead boy, "Son, get up." The lad sits up and starts talking. Jesus gives him back to his mom.

Jesus doesn't act because of the woman's faith or at her request. He acts because he has compassion for her and her loss. Jesus raises her son from the dead. He performs a miracle for this woman's benefit, in her best interest.

Though Jesus didn't raise every dead person during his time on earth, he did raise some.

Do we believe Jesus is able to do amazing things for us today?

[Discover more about the widow from Nain in Luke 7:11–17.]

The Daughter of Jairus

J airus is a leader at the local synagogue. His twelve-year-old daughter is gravely ill. He comes to Jesus and begs the Rabbi to heal his little girl. Jesus agrees, but he's delayed along the way when he stops to heal a hemorrhaging woman. Then word comes to Jairus that it's too late. His daughter is dead.

Jesus ignores their words and tells Jairus to just believe. Apparently Jairus does.

When Jesus arrives at Jairus's house, the mourning for his daughter's passing has already begun. Dismissing the crowd, he leads her parents and three disciples to her body. He takes the dead girl's hand and tells her to get up. Much to everyone's shock, she does. Then she walks around, very much alive.

We don't know what this girl experienced in the spiritual realm when she was dead or what her life in the physical realm was like afterwards. But she must certainly have lived with an appreciation for her father's strong faith and the knowledge that her second chance at life is because of Jesus's power over death.

She experienced Jesus's healing power, in part, because of the faith of her father. Do we have that kind of faith today?

[Discover more about Jairus's daughter in Mark 5:22–43 and Luke 8:40–56.]

The Hemorrhaging Woman

A woman suffers from chronic bleeding for twelve years, making her ceremonially unclean the entire time. According to Jewish law, this condition restricts how she functions in society and prohibits her from participating in religious practices. She spends all her money on doctors, but none of them help. Instead, her bleeding gets worse.

In desperation, but with great faith, she believes Jesus can heal her.

In fact, she senses she need only touch his clothes. She worms her way through the throng and stretches out her hand to brush the hem of his robe. When she does, healing power leaves him, and her bleeding stops. Her body is restored.

Though she thinks she does this in secret, Jesus is aware that healing took place. He stops and demands to know who touched him. Unable to escape, she comes forward in fear to confess what she did.

Jesus affirms her faith, pronounces her healed, and sends her away in peace.

Do we have this kind of faith?

[Discover more about the bleeding woman in Mark 5:25–34 and Luke 8:43–48, as well as the Old Testament instructions about this situation Leviticus 15:25–30.]

The Queen of the South

Jesus criticizes the people for not realizing who he is. He calls them an evil generation. He alludes to the queen of the south (the queen of Sheba), who, after hearing about King Solomon's reputation, comes to check things out for herself, traveling a great distance and giving him many gifts. She is not disappointed with what she sees and hears.

Now Jesus—who is much greater than King Solomon—stands before them, but they fail to seek him with the same earnestness that the queen of the south sought Solomon.

They don't understand. Jesus, I think, is miffed.

The queen of the south made an extraordinary effort to discover the truth about King Solomon. Are we willing to put forth the same effort to seek Jesus?

[Discover more about the queen of the south in Luke 11:29–31. See "The Queen of Sheba" for the backstory in the Old Testament section.]

A Woman in the Crowd

As Jesus speaks, a woman in the throng is so mesmerized by his words that she yells the first thing that comes to mind. It comes out something like, "Your mom rocks!" I think she's trying to affirm him and honor the mother who raised him.

Jesus responds indirectly. He says that even better are people who hear what God says and obey him. This puts things in perspective.

The woman, enthralled by Jesus, attempts to communicate her enthusiasm. But she misses the main point: obeying God is what matters most.

In our zeal for Jesus, how often have we said or done something that was off base from what he wants from us?

[Discover more about the woman in the crowd in Luke 11:27–28.]

The Crippled Woman

A woman is disabled, so much so that she is perpetually bent over and can't begin to stand straight. She has endured this for eighteen years.

When Jesus sees her, he reaches out and touches her crippled form. Immediately the bones in her body re-align. She stands up straight, thanking God.

A religious leader who sees this happen should have joined in on the celebration. Instead he criticizes Jesus because this healing happened on their day of rest, the Sabbath. The misguided leader thinks his traditions and religious rules are more important than helping people in need.

Jesus thinks otherwise and sets him straight.

This woman becomes the center of controversy, not for what she does but because a religious leader tries to use her to advance his own agenda.

Have we ever judged a person or their situation when we should have offered love instead?

[Discover more about the disabled woman in Luke 13:10–17.]

The Woman Who Lost Her Coin

J esus shares a story to instruct the people.

There's a woman who has ten pieces of silver. She misplaces one of them. You'd think she'd be more careful, but she wasn't. Due to her negligence, she loses 10 percent of her funds. This isn't a paper loss when the stock market drops. This is real money. One tenth of her wealth is gone.

Panicked, she lights a lamp and carefully searches the floor. To her relief, she finds the lost coin. She lets everyone know about her good fortune, and they share in her delight. She even throws a party.

Then Jesus makes his point. There's an even greater celebration when someone turns their life around to follow God.

How excited do we get when someone decides to follow Jesus?

[Discover more about the woman who lost her coin in Luke 15:8–10.]

The Persistent Widow

Later Jesus uses another story to instruct the people about God and prayer.

This time he tells them of a widow who has received unfair treatment. She goes to the judge seeking justice. But the unscrupulous judge ignores her appeals for help. Despite him dismissing her, she keeps coming before him, over and over. She's so intense that he begins to fear for his safety.

Eventually she wears him down.

Even though he cares nothing about her plight or doing what's right, he decides to help her just so she'll stop bugging him. In the end, he makes sure she receives the ruling she sought all along.

This, Jesus says, is an illustration to keep praying for what we need. If an unjust judge will answer a woman's pleas, how much more will a just God answer ours?

Do we ask God once and stop, or are we persistent when we pray?

[Discover more about the persistent widow in Luke 18:1–8.]

The Poor Widow and
Her Offering

Jesus and his disciples stand near the temple as people come to give their money. One poor woman drops in two small copper coins. Her offering is so small. Surely it will do no good, unlike the considerable gifts of all the others.

Jesus sees things differently.

He pronounces her gift, though numerically small, as greater than everyone else's. Then he explains. While they gave out of their abundance, she gave out of her poverty—all she had to live on.

God doesn't consider the size of the gift as much as the intent of the giver.

How does God view our gifts?

[Discover more about the poor woman's offering in Mark 12:41–44 and Luke 21:1–4.]

The Canaanite Woman / The Syrophoenician Woman

Jesus hangs out in Tyre, trying to rest, but folks track him down. One of the people who comes to him for help is a foreign woman. While Matthew states she is from Canaan, Mark says she is a Greek, born in Syrian Phoenicia. Some people call her a Syrophoenician. Regardless of where she's from, the key point is that she isn't Jewish.

She has a little girl with a big issue. The girl's possessed by an impure spirit. The mom begs Jesus to heal her daughter by driving out the demon within her.

Jesus dismisses the woman. He says what the people expect, insinuating he came only to help Jewish people, not foreigners. In doing so, he implies she's a dog, trying to eat the children's food. What he's really doing is creating a teachable moment.

She does not accept his rebuff.

His apparent ethnic judgment doesn't offend her. She is quick to counter, noting that even the dogs eat the crumbs that fall from the children's table.

Jesus affirms her wise reply. He pronounces the little girl healed. Now the people should realize that Jesus is here for both Jews and Gentiles. But they don't.

When Mom gets home, her daughter is resting in bed. The demon is gone.

When we encounter a rebuff, do we accept it and give up or try even harder to achieve our goal? When God doesn't seem to listen to our pleas for help, do we stop asking or persist?

[Discover more about this woman in Matthew 15:21–28 and Mark 7:24–30.]

The Adulterous Woman

J esus's detractors drag a woman caught in the act of adultery before him. The religious leaders who present her care nothing about her, what she did, or justice. If they have true concern for the law they claim to uphold, they would have likewise offered up her adulterous partner along with her.

Instead they are exploiting her to try to trap Jesus into saying something they can use against him. Being knowledgeable about Scripture, as well as their made-up rules about religion, they are sure they can twist whatever Jesus says to ruin him.

The woman is merely their pawn.

Jesus refuses to take sides, something her accusers had not considered. Had he either upheld the law or offered her mercy, they could have used it against him. Instead he thwarts their devious scheme. Without pronouncing judgment, he allows anyone who is perfect to begin the prescribed punishment of execution by stoning. The person who is without sin may throw the first rock. No one qualifies, and they slink away.

Once they all leave, Jesus offers the woman mercy and lets her go. He encourages her to change her behavior.

Too often, well-meaning religious leaders are quick to condemn others when they should extend love and encouragement.

Is our nature to judge others or offer them love and mercy? What would Jesus do?

[Discover more about this woman in John 8:1–11.]

Mary (2) Magdalene

Recent public opinion about Mary Magdalene has not been kind, with people making unfounded assumptions about her. Some think she's a prostitute or accuse her of an immoral lifestyle, but we don't find that in the Bible. What Scripture does say is that Jesus cast seven demons out of her. Regardless of how we understand this, we know that Jesus makes her life much better.

In response, Mary Magdalene shows her gratitude by following Jesus and helping to support him financially. She's also there, along with a few other women, when Jesus dies and later when he's buried. The next day, Mary Magdalene leads a group to his tomb to properly prepare his body, according to the customs of the day.

Of course, they can't do this because Jesus isn't there. Angels at the grave tell her Jesus has risen from the dead, that he is alive. Later Jesus appears to her and tells her to let the disciples know.

This is significant, as two-thousand years ago a woman's testimony wasn't legally accepted, but to underscore God's affirmation of women, he has them deliver the breaking news of the most significant event in human history. This makes a female the first apostle after Jesus's death.

Like Mary Magdalene, people sometimes think or say things about us that aren't true. While this can hurt deeply, it's God's opinion that counts.

What people say about us shouldn't matter, but does it? Is our conscience clear before God?

[Discover more about Mary Magdalene in Matthew 27:55–28:10, Luke 8:1–3, Luke 24:1–10, John 19:25, and John 20:1–18.]

Martha

Martha is the sister of Mary and Lazarus, whom Jesus raises from the dead. Though Jesus loves all people, the Bible specifically mentions that he loves Martha and her two siblings.

In reading what Luke and John write about Martha, we can draw several conclusions: She owns her own home. She likes to entertain and has the gift of hospitality. Her love language is acts of service. And she may be older than her brother and sister.

Scripture shares two stories about Martha. In one, she offers the most profound, faith-filled testimony about Jesus: "I believe you're the Messiah, the Son of God, who has come into the world." Her boldness and confidence are inspiring. She declares this shortly before Jesus faces his execution. Unfortunately, this is not what we best remember Martha for.

The other story happens earlier in her life. She invites Jesus and his friends over for a meal. Amid her busy preparations, she complains to Jesus that her sister, Mary, isn't helping to get the food ready. Instead, Mary is hanging out with Jesus.

In Jesus's surprising response, he affirms Mary as doing the best thing she can do and tells Martha she needs to calm down. This perplexes me because if Martha followed her sister's example, no one would have anything to eat.

Another consideration, however, is Martha's misguided assumption that Mary should go along with her plans to feed Jesus. It is Martha's choice to invite Jesus over. Mary doesn't make that offer and has no obligation to help. Both sisters show their commitment to Jesus. They just do it differently.

How often do we expect others to automatically go along with our grand ideas or commitments? Do we get mad when they don't help us as we think they should?

[Discover more about Martha in Luke 10:38–42, John 11:5–44, and John 12:2–7.]

Mary (3), Martha and Lazarus's Sister

M ary is the sister of Martha and Lazarus. The Bible includes two stories about her that cause me to label her as irresponsible. Jesus, however, has a different perspective.

In the first story, Mary sits at the feet of Jesus, taking in all he says and basking in his presence while her sister, Martha, toils in the kitchen. Martha complains about Mary's laziness, but Jesus puts Martha in her place, and he affirms Mary for making the better choice.

In the second story, Mary uses some expensive perfume, which she pours on Jesus's feet and wipes them with her hair, to show her love to him and symbolically prepare him for burial.

Judas criticizes her wasteful ways. He claims the perfume is worth one year's salary. Instead of pouring it on Jesus, a better use would have been to sell it and use the proceeds to help the poor. But Jesus rebuffs Judas, saying Mary did the right thing with her perfume, the thing she was meant to do.

Mary first faces criticism for being lazy and later for being wasteful. But Jesus commends both her choices.

Do we ever judge others from a human standpoint and completely miss God's perspective?

[Discover more about Mary in Luke 10:38–42 and John 12:2–7. See "The Women Who Anoint Jesus."]

The Samaritan Woman
at the Well

The Jews dismiss Samaritans as half-breed misfits. They refuse to associate with them. Even talking to one is social suicide. Yet Jesus defies convention and purposefully travels to their town and even rests there. While he waits at the local well, he sends his disciples into town to buy food.

At noon, a Samaritan woman comes to draw water. She may pick this time of day to avoid being there with the other women of the village. Her life choices make her an outcast. She's an outcast among outcasts.

Jesus surprises her by asking for a drink of water. She's shocked. Not only is he breaking conventions in talking with a detested Samaritan and a woman, but he asks for a favor. If she gives him water, he will need to drink from her cup, another thing completely unacceptable to Jews.

Jesus, however, doesn't care what others think. He cares for her.

He also knows about her past, that she's been married five times and isn't married to the guy she's living with. Amazed that he knows her secrets, she affirms him as a prophet and later learns he is the Messiah everyone has been waiting for.

She goes and tells the villagers what Jesus said. Based on her testimony, they come out to meet him and believe in him. They ask him to hang out with them and he stays for two days.

When we tell others about Jesus, is our story compelling enough for them to seriously consider him?

[Discover more about the Samaritan woman in John 4:5–42.]

The Wife of Pilate

A key player in Jesus's execution is the governor, Pilate. The religious leaders, jealous because of Jesus's growing popularity and his influence over the people, take him to Pilate. They ask for his approval to kill Jesus.

Pilate, aware of their motives, wants to free Jesus, but the leaders stir up the crowd and a riot threatens to erupt. As Pilate considers what to do, his wife sends him a cryptic message, confirming Jesus's innocence and warning Pilate to not have anything to do with him. She implies Pilate will endure great personal suffering if he isn't careful.

Unable to control the crowd and unwilling to stand up to them, Pilate dismisses his wife's sage warning and agrees to let them kill Jesus. He could have stopped them, but he didn't.

Our spouses, family, and close friends can help us avoid trouble and not make wrong decisions. Are we willing to listen?

[Discover more about Pilate's wife in Matthew 27:11–26.]

Salome

Salome is a follower of Jesus, one of several women who help support him and his ministry. She's also one of a small group of women who are brave enough to attempt to embalm Jesus's body after he's crucified. But they don't get to do this because he's already risen from the dead by the time they arrive at his tomb.

Of the four biographers of Jesus, only Mark mentions Salome, though Luke may implicitly include her with the phrase "and many others." What is clear is that a group of women provide key assistance to Jesus and his squad, offering both money and food. Salome, one of these women, receives only one brief mention of her critical involvement in Jesus's work here on earth—and a second one for her desire to respect his body after his execution.

Receiving minimal recognition, however, doesn't diminish the key role she plays.

We may not receive credit here on earth for the things we do for Jesus, but that doesn't make our actions and sacrifices any less significant.

[Discover more about Salome in Mark 15:40–41, Mark 16:1, and Luke 8:3.]

Mary (4) the Mother of James and Joseph

There are many women named Mary in the New Testament of the Bible. One is identified by the names of her boys: Mary, the mother of James and Joseph. This Mary is one of a handful of women noted for following Jesus and caring for his needs. Like Salome, Joanna, and Susanna, we acknowledge Mary's key role in Jesus's ministry.

Referring to her as Mary the mother of James and Joseph may clarify her to first-century audiences, but it doesn't help us much today, as we can only speculate who her sons are. However, it's reasonable to assume her sons are noteworthy in the early church, which is commendable to her for raising godly boys.

Our children may be our biggest and most important legacy. May we do everything possible to raise them into godly men and women.

[Discover more about this Mary in Matthew 27:55–56, Mark 15:40–41, Mark 16:1, and Luke 24:1–11.]

The Mother of James and John

Two of Jesus's disciples are James and John. Their mother comes to Jesus, making an audacious request for her boys. She asks that Jesus honor them by letting them sit on his right and his left in his kingdom.

Jesus is direct. "You don't realize what you're asking." Eventually he says only his Father can grant such a request. The other disciples are peeved at the brothers and their mom for being so pushy.

However, we later see her bravely keeping vigil at the cross as Jesus dies. Matthew notes that she's one of the women who follows Jesus and cares for him. But we remember her most for being a pushy mom and her shameless promotion of her sons.

How can we know when to advocate for our children and when to let them grow up and fend for themselves?

[Discover more about James and John's mother in Matthew 20:20–28 and Matthew 27:55–56.]

The Women Who Anoint Jesus

Each of the four accounts of Jesus's life—in Matthew, Mark, Luke, and John—give a story about a woman who anoints Jesus with expensive perfume, but the details in each narrative vary a bit. It may be that this happens on four separate occasions. Or it could be the same story, with a few details that differ. Or perhaps it is somewhere in between, with there being two or three times that women anoint Jesus.

Matthew and Mark's accounts are the closest, with the only differing detail being who criticizes her for wasting expensive perfume on Jesus: Matthew says it's the disciples. Mark says it's "some" people. Matthew and Mark likely cover the same event.

In John's version, the woman who anoints Jesus is Mary (3), sister of Martha and Lazarus, but for the other three reports, the woman isn't named. John's version is like Matthew and Mark's, but one key difference is that this woman anoints Jesus's feet, not his head, as in the first two accounts. Also, John identifies just one person who criticizes her: Judas Iscariot. Last, John says that Martha is serving the dinner in Jesus's honor, so we assume it is at her house, whereas Matthew and Mark say Jesus is hanging out at Simon the leper's home.

Of the four writers, John is the only one who is an eyewitness, whereas the others needed to research their account. However, John is the last one to write it down, so it's hard to say if he got the part about the feet, along with the other details, right or wrong. Regardless, it's reasonable to assume he's telling the same story as Matthew and Mark.

In all three accounts Jesus defends the woman's action and says she is preparing him for burial.

Luke's version differs the most from the other three. First, he calls her a sinful woman, something not even hinted at in the other accounts. Also, she crashes the party. Next, this takes place at a Pharisee's house. His name is Simon, but it doesn't say he's a leper. And there's no mention of it being in the town of Bethany. A woman comes up behind Jesus and weeps at his feet, apparently in sorrow for her wayward ways. Her tears fall on him and, lacking a towel, she uses her hair to dry his feet. Then she dumps her perfume on them.

In this account, the woman doesn't receive criticism, but Jesus does. The Pharisee thinks that Jesus should have known the woman touching him is a sinner.

Jesus affirms the woman for washing his feet, something his host declined to do. Then he forgives her for her many sins, affirms her saving faith, and sends her off in peace. Luke's account contains enough differences that it's likely a different event.

Although some people, like myself, enjoy digging this deeply into the Bible, we should do so loosely. It doesn't really matter if this story is about one woman, or two, or three, or four. What counts is that it happened. The specific details don't matter so much. When we read Scripture as narrative, the way it's written, we can enjoy this story and receive inspiration through it. However, if we see Scripture as merely an irrefutable historical treatise, then we'll surely trip over the minutia.

The key point is that these women give us an example of lavish adoration of Jesus.

How exuberant is our worship of Jesus? Are we free to worship him regardless of what others say or think?

[Discover more about the four stories of women who anoint Jesus in Matthew 26:6–13, Mark 14:3–9, Luke 7:36–50, and John 12:1–8.]

Joanna

Just as Salome only appears in Mark's biography of Jesus, Joanna receives mention only in Luke's. However, the two should know each other, as they both help care for Jesus and support his work.

Joanna also joins Mary Magdalene and Mary the mother of James and Joseph in wanting to embalm Jesus's body, which they don't get to do. He has already risen from the dead before they get their chance.

A third thing we know about Joanna is that, along with Mary Magdalene and Susanna, Jesus casts demons out of her. Whether we understand demon possession as a spiritual condition or first century man's understanding of mental illness doesn't matter.

The key is that Jesus relieves her of her affliction. Her response is to do what she can for him.

Today we look to Jesus to save us, but do we also look to him to heal us? He came to do both.

[Discover more about Joanna in Luke 8:2–3 and Luke 24:1–11.]

Susanna (2)

S usanna is only mentioned once in the Bible. It's by Doctor Luke in his biography of Jesus. Jesus casts a demon out of her, as he does for Joanna and many others. Regardless of what we understand this to mean, Susanna, in response to Jesus removing her affliction, helps support him and his work here on earth.

While Jesus doesn't demand we do things for him out of gratitude for what he does for us, he certainly deserves our tangible acts of appreciation.

What do we do to show Jesus our love for him?

[Discover more about Susanna in Luke 8:2–3.]

Mary (5) the wife of Clopas

Another woman named Mary is identified by her husband's name: Mary the wife of Clopas. Only one verse in the Bible, in John's biography of Jesus, contains a reference to this Mary or mentions Clopas. While we may bristle at the idea of Mary's identity being tied to her husband, this may be more a notation of convenience rather than significance. While Clopas did nothing noteworthy, Mary did.

When all the disciples, except John, abandon Jesus as he dies a slow death by crucifixion, four women are brave enough to remain close by, keeping vigil as Jesus suffers. They stay near him despite great personal risk, something the rest of his followers are unwilling to do.

One of these courageous women is Mary, the wife of Clopas. We salute her for staying by Jesus and supporting him in his darkest moment.

What have we done for Jesus? What else can we do?

[Discover more about Mary, the wife of Clopas, in John 19:25.]

Aunt of Jesus

It's reasonable to assume Jesus's mother, Mary, has brothers and sisters, but only one appears in the Bible. It's Mary's sister, which would be Jesus's aunt. Yes, Jesus has an aunt. We don't know her name, and she garners only one brief mention, but what she does is significant.

Though we can only speculate if Mary's sister is a follower of Jesus, we do know that she stands by her sister's side while Mary keeps her vigil as Jesus dies.

That's what family does. That's what friends do. They stand by us in our darkest moments, perhaps saying nothing, just being present.

Do we have these deep kinds of friendships? Are we this type of devoted friend to others?

[Discover more about Jesus's aunt in John 19:25.]

The Other Mary (6)

Matthew twice mentions "the other Mary." Who is this other woman named Mary? Since he also mentions Mary Magdalene in those verses, we know it's not her. It's also doubtful that he would refer to Jesus's mother with such a vague reference. It's also unlikely that she's Mary the mother of James and Joseph because Matthew mentions that Mary elsewhere in his writings.

A possibility is that "the other Mary" could refer to Mary the wife of Clopas, whom Matthew doesn't mention. The same applies for Mary, the sister of Martha and Lazarus, or she could be Mary the mother of John Mark.

It's also possible she's another Mary altogether.

What we do know is this Mary, along with Mary Magdalene, watches Joseph entomb Jesus. The next day they return to his grave.

Why do we bother to have all these considerations over someone we can't identify?

"The other Mary" reminds us that sometimes we don't receive credit for the things we do. Or that our actions may receive only a vague nod. But Jesus knows. That's what matters.

How willing are we to serve Jesus if no one else were to know what we do?

[Discover more about this Mary in Matthew 27:61 and Matthew 28:1.]

Sapphira

S apphira and her husband sell some land and give part of the proceeds to the church. They keep some of it for themselves, which they're free to do, but they say their donation is the full amount of the sale.

Peter confronts Sapphira's husband about his duplicity. The man drops dead. There's no mercy offered, no second chance given, and no investigation conducted. In this case, God's judgment is swift. It's final.

Later, not knowing the fate of her husband, Sapphira shows up, and Peter confronts her as well. Again, there's no mercy, second chance, or investigation. She, too, falls dead. A holy fear grips the church.

We seldom suffer immediate punishment for the wrong things we do. This delay could cause us to assume judgment won't happen, but without Jesus's saving power, punishment is inevitable.

Sapphira and her husband conspire to deceive the church, but more significantly, they lie to the Holy

Spirit. In their case, lying to the Holy Spirit is punishable by death, an immediate death.

How might we lie to the Holy Spirit?

[Discover more about Sapphira in Act 5:1–11.]

Queen Candace

Candace is the queen of Ethiopia. That's all we know about her. Some translations don't even give her name, but instead call her the Kandake, which means *the queen of Ethiopia*. An important member of her cabinet, the treasurer, is in Jerusalem to worship God. Returning to Ethiopia in his chariot, he reads from Isaiah's prophecy but has trouble understanding it.

Meanwhile, God directs Philip into the desert for an undisclosed reason. As Philip walks along the arid trail, he meets the Ethiopian treasurer. Philip explains that the confusing passage refers to Jesus and tells the man who Jesus is and what he did.

The man receives Philip's teaching about Jesus. When they come to some water, he asks Philip to baptize him. Philip does. Then he's whisked away by the Holy Spirit, while the man continues his journey home, overflowing with joy. When he gets there, I suspect he tells everyone about Jesus.

We see Candace as a wise leader, allowing one of her most trusted lieutenants time off for religious reasons. As a result, he returns a changed man, which likely influences his work, the government, and the nation in a positive way.

It's easy for us to envision him telling Queen Candace about Jesus, but we're left to wonder how she responds.

Who can we tell about Jesus?

[Discover more about Queen Candace in Acts 8:26–40.]

Tabitha (Dorcas)

Tabitha, also known as Dorcas, is a good person. She enjoys helping those who are less fortunate, often making them clothes.

She gets sick and dies.

Her friends and neighbors prepare her body for burial. They mourn her death, while celebrating her life.

Peter's in a nearby town. Some faith-filled followers of Jesus send for him to come as soon as possible. Peter arrives and goes to where they've laid her body for viewing. He looks at her and tells her to get up. She does. He guides her to the balcony and presents her to all those who are paying their respects.

News of this amazing miracle spreads fast. As a result, many more people believe in Jesus.

Tabitha dedicated her life to helping people in need, but, like Jesus, it was her death and resurrection that helped them the most.

Does our life, and will our death, point people to Jesus? What must change?

[Discover more about Tabitha in Acts 9:36–42.]

Mary (7) the Mother of John Mark

In the book of Acts, we come across another Mary. The Bible clarifies her identity through the name of her son: John, also called Mark. Scripture sometimes uses both names, as in John Mark.

Peter is in prison, with his execution likely. Mary—risking imprisonment herself if she's discovered—bravely holds a prayer meeting for Peter at her home. God answers the prayers of the believers, and an angel escorts Peter from the prison. Peter heads to Mary's house, expecting to find some of his friends gathered there. They welcome him and celebrate God's goodness.

Though we can only assume, John Mark witnesses his mother's faith in action and God's supernatural answer to their prayers. What we do know is that John Mark later helps tell other people about Jesus. Though his first effort with Barnabas and Paul ends prematurely, he finishes strong. Many people credit him as the author of the book of Mark.

Children watch what we do and say. What are they learning from us?

[Discover more about John Mark's mother, Mary, in Acts 12:12–16.]

Rhoda

Rhoda is present at the prayer meeting for Peter when he's sitting in jail and facing execution. Rhoda is a servant, likely of Mary, the mother of John Mark, at whose house the people meet to pray. From the story we gather that Rhoda is also a follower of Jesus, interceding for Peter along with everyone else.

During the meeting, there's a knock on the door. As part of her duties, Rhoda goes to the door. She asks who's there. Peter identifies himself. Overjoyed at hearing his voice, Rhoda runs to tell everyone the good news, but she forgets to let Peter in.

The people, despite their intense focus on praying for Peter, don't believe God answered their prayers. Though they're praying for a miracle, they fear the worst. It's only after Peter's continued knocking that they let him in and discover the truth. Once they see him, they finally realize God's amazing answer to their prayers.

Unlike the others present, Rhoda prays with expectation. Merely hearing Peter's voice is all the evidence she needs. Everyone else doubts. Their faith is weak.

When we pray, do we pray in faith with expectation or in doubt out of fear?

[Discover more about Rhoda in Acts 12:12–16.]

Lydia

Lydia is a merchant who sells expensive purple material. She lives in Philippi. She worships God, but she doesn't know about Jesus. When Paul shows up, he tells her who Jesus is and what he did. She decides to follow Jesus too. She's baptized to show her commitment. Then she asks Paul and his buddies to come over and hang out at her house.

Later, Paul and Silas heal a fortune-telling slave girl and end up in jail as a result. The next day they're released and head back to Lydia's house where they meet with more of Jesus's followers. After giving them some encouragement, Paul and Silas leave town.

When Lydia decides to follow Jesus, she goes all in. She even has people meet at her house. She doesn't need to take a class, join a church, or wait until her faith matures. She does what she can right away.

We later learn of an active local church in Philippi. I imagine Lydia is a key part of it. They may even meet at her house.

Do we make people wait before we let them serve Jesus or help in our church?

[Discover more about Lydia in Acts 16:14–40.]

The Fortune Teller

When Paul and Silas are in Philippi, they encounter a slave girl who possesses the psychic ability to tell people's fortunes. Using her fortune-telling skills, she earns a great deal of money for her owners.

When she sees Paul, the spirit within her proclaims supernatural truth: "These men are from God Most High. They're telling everyone how to get saved." She continues this day after day, until Paul grows exasperated.

Evoking Jesus's name, Paul commands the fortune-telling spirit to leave her. The spirit obeys, and the girl loses the ability to tell people their future.

She's now free of her controlling spirit. Though we don't know what happens to her after this, we do know what happens to Paul and Silas. They spend a night in jail for their trouble.

The slave girl is exploited by her owners and spiritually freed by Jesus, through Paul's boldness.

Who does Jesus want us to help free?

[Discover more about the fortune teller in Acts 16:16–19.]

Artemis

The people in Ephesus worship the goddess Artemis. Though history tells us much about her, the Bible doesn't. Looking only at the biblical text, we see her as a character of mythological stature, either a complete work of fiction or a blatant distortion of someone who once was. The people have elevated her to the status of god, and the tradespeople have built businesses around her.

The silversmith Demetrius is one such person. He crafts silver shrines, which he sells to people who worship her. Demetrius cares nothing about Artemis, only the profits he can earn by exploiting her notoriety. He even acknowledges she is a made-up god, void of divinity. Yet he seeks to uphold her legend for personal gain, opposing Paul—and ultimately Jesus—in the process. Demetrius doesn't want to see her discredited in any way, for his financial future depends on her.

He resorts to rhetoric. His zealous speech stirs up a mob. The agitated crowd yells for a couple of hours.

The situation threatens to turn into a riot. At last the city clerk quiets the crowd and restores civil obedience.

They misuse the memory of Artemis to mislead people and generate income, exploiting her for personal gain.

How have we ever exploited a person, or their memory, to maintain power or earn a profit?

[Discover more about Artemis in Acts 19:23–41.]

Eunice

E unice is the mother of Timothy, who, as Paul's protégé, grows in his faith to help others grow in theirs. Though we know the results of Eunice's character as reflected in her son, we know little about her.

She's only mentioned twice in the Bible. She's Jewish and believes in Jesus. However, contrary to Jewish law, she married a non-Jew. This puts her on the outside of Jewish society, causing true Jews to shun her or look down on her. She also doesn't circumcise her son, as required by Jewish law. However, despite the ramifications of who she marries, we also know she has a real faith, which she learned from her mother and passes on to her son.

Our faith is the greatest thing we can give to our children. Are we doing all we can?

[Discover more about Eunice in Acts 16:1 and 2 Timothy 1:5.]

Damaris

Damaris is another woman whose name only appears once in the Bible. And we know only one thing about her. After Paul tells a group of people about Jesus, she believes.

Luke writes that in addition to Damaris, Dionysius also believes, along with many others. But why is Damaris's name recorded and most of the other new believers aren't? We don't know, but Luke must think it's important we know that Damaris believes in Jesus.

While Damaris's name is written in Scripture, Jesus says the names of others who serve him are written in heaven. Paul says the same thing. John warns about people whose names aren't written in Jesus's book of life and later commends those who are.

Although our name will never appear in the Bible, it can still be written in heaven and appear in Jesus's book of life. Does yours?

[Discover more about Damaris in Acts 17:34. Also see Luke 10:20, Hebrews 12:23, Revelation 13:8, and Revelation 21:27.]

The Sister of Paul

We know little about Paul's family. All we can learn about him from Scripture is that he is a bachelor and has a sister and nephew. His nephew stumbles upon a conspiracy to kill Paul, alerts him, and then tells the authorities. They protect Paul, saving him from certain death at the hands of forty men committed to killing him.

Had they been successful, Paul's ministry would have been cut in half and most of his letters to the churches would never have been written. Our Bible would be much shorter, and Christianity would have been much different, if not for a young boy who did the right thing despite personal risk. It's a good thing Paul's sister raised her son well and taught him to do the right thing.

Though we thank Paul for his contributions to the Bible and our faith, we should also thank Paul's nephew and sister who made his ongoing work possible. (In contrast, for a sister who didn't support her sibling's ministry, consider Miriam when she opposed her brother, Moses.)

Whether it's a family member or close friend, being in the shadow of someone who is well-known or accomplished is never easy. Common reactions are envy, bitterness, or a diminished self-worth. Yet the small things we do, even though they go largely unnoticed, can help our relative or friend accomplish even more. We can contribute, behind the scenes, to their success.

What family member can we help to achieve better results?

[Discover more about Paul's sister in Acts 23:12–24. Also see Numbers 12.]

Drusilla

Drusilla is the wife of the governor, Felix. She is Jewish. Apparently, he isn't. Paul is in jail, under the jurisdiction of Felix. Felix listens to Paul talk about his faith in Jesus, but despite a stirring within, the governor is afraid to make a commitment.

He could release Paul, but instead he keeps him in jail, hoping for a bribe. Two years later, when Felix is replaced as governor, Paul still languishes in prison.

Spouses influence one another. Drusilla could have encouraged her husband to do the right thing and free Paul. Though we don't know if she tried or not, we do know that Felix didn't release Paul.

Each of us can influence others. Are we doing all we can to inspire them to do good?

[Discover more about Drusilla in Acts 24:24–27.]

Bernice

Each time we see Bernice in the Bible, she's paired with King Agrippa. Though Scripture doesn't state their relationship, history does. They're siblings.

The pair become involved in determining the fate of the imprisoned Paul. Throughout this story, we see Bernice as a partner to the king, accompanying him to events, sitting in on Paul's hearing, and being part of the follow-up meeting.

After listening to Paul present his case, the pair, along with others, adjourns to discuss his situation. Bernice takes part in reaching the group's conclusion that Paul has not done anything to deserve the severe penalty his detractors seek.

Whether a spouse, relative, or valued friend, God puts people in our lives who can work with us, support and encourage us, and help us make wise decisions.

Are we doing all we can to help those around us? Are we listening to those God has placed in our lives?

[Discover more about Bernice in Acts 25:13, 23 and Acts 26:30–31.]

Lois

Paul refers to Lois, Timothy's grandmother, as having a sincere faith in God. She passes this on to her daughter Eunice. Eunice, in turn, passes her beliefs on to her son Timothy. While we don't know if Timothy has any children to teach his faith to, we do know that in his role as a missionary and church leader, he influences many others to grow in theirs.

Lois instills her faith in her daughter, the most significant thing she can do. As a result, two generations later, her grandson travels around the area to help others grow in their trust in God.

Even if we only influence one person to grow in their faith, we have no idea who else they may help. The only way we influence no one—now or in the future—is if we keep our faith a secret.

Who are we passing our faith to?

[Discover more about Lois in 2 Timothy 1:5.]

Priscilla

Exiled from Rome, Priscilla and her husband, Aquila, are missionaries who work with local churches and help other missionaries. Tentmakers, like Paul, they first meet him in Corinth where they work together. Later they travel to Syria and then to Ephesus. As Paul journeys on, Priscilla and Aquila stay in Ephesus to help that church.

In Ephesus they meet Apollos. An educated man, he tells others about God with much zeal, but he only knows about the baptism of John. So Priscilla and Aquila tell him the full story of Jesus. Then Apollos goes out on his own to tell others about this good news.

In his letters, Paul calls Priscilla and Aquila his co-workers, confirms they risked their lives for him, and affirms that the churches appreciate their work.

Later Priscilla and Aquila are back in Rome when Paul writes to that church, and they are with Timothy when Paul sends his second letter to the young preacher. However, when Paul sends his second letter to the church in Corinth, Priscilla and Aquila are with him. At some point they start a house church, but Scripture doesn't tell us where.

The Bible always mentions Priscilla and Aquila together, never as individuals. What's interesting is that contrary to the cultural norm of listing the husband, Aquila, first and the wife second, Priscilla usually appears first and then Aquila. We could assume this means Priscilla takes a lead role in their work. Another understanding is Priscilla's name appears first to confirm she isn't secondary to her husband. Instead they are truly equal partners, sharing leadership roles as needed. In this way they can best help the church of Jesus grow.

If we serve God with our spouse, do we work as equal partners, or does one person lead and receive all the credit?

[Discover more about Priscilla in Acts 18:1–26, Romans 16:3–4, 1 Corinthians 16:19, and 2 Timothy 4:19.]

The Daughters of Philip

P hilip, full of God's spirit, is skilled at telling people about Jesus. He also has four daughters, who all possess the spiritual gift of prophecy. That is, they can accurately predict the future through the power of God's Holy Spirit.

The Bible tells us nothing more about these four amazing girls, but their spiritual abilities likely stem from their father's faith and their own willingness to follow Jesus and be empowered by his Holy Spirit.

It's a great tribute to parents when their children follow Jesus and even more so when he uses them in powerful ways.

How are we preparing our children and those we teach to receive and then use God's supernatural power?

[Discover more about Philip's four daughters in Acts 21:8–9.]

Phoebe

Paul wraps up his letter to the Romans by mentioning a string of people, several of them women. First up is Phoebe, a church deacon. Paul commends her and sends her to Rome as a missionary. He tells the people there to assist her in every way possible. Paul ends by affirming that she has helped many other people, including himself.

For those who think women can't serve in church leadership or as a lone missionary, Phoebe's example shows us it wasn't always this way, especially in the beginning. Paul's affirmation of her confirms he places no restrictions on how a woman can serve God.

Paul lauds Phoebe as a deacon, a missionary, and a huge help to others. Through his writing, we know these things about her.

What are we known for? Are our work and character worth people writing about?

[Discover more about Phoebe in Romans 16:1–2.]

Mary (8)

The next female on Paul's list is Mary. She could be one of the other seven Marys we've already covered, but this would mean that she moved to Rome and became part of that church. This is unlikely, so we can assume she's another Mary.

We know one thing about her. She works hard for the church in Rome. Though she lacks the title of deacon, like Phoebe, she nonetheless serves with noteworthy diligence.

Do we work hard for God or hardly work?

[Discover more about this Mary in Romans 16:6.]

Junia

Next on his list, Paul says to say, "Hi," to Andronicus and Junia. We know four things about this pair: they are Jewish, they are in prison, they are standout apostles, and they are Christians. One thing that's not clear is if Junia is a man or a woman.

Though it's speculation, I think Junia is female, and she's married to Andronicus. They are a team, a successful husband and wife missionary team.

What we can learn from Junia is that gender doesn't matter, character does. Some people have names that mask their gender, voices that result in wrong assumptions, or even appearances that confuse.

Though others may assume wrong things about us, God focuses on our character and what we do.

Are we doing what God calls us to, regardless of what others think?

[Discover more about Junia in Romans 16:7.]

Tryphena and Tryphosa

Tryphena and Tryphosa may be sisters or they could be friends, but the key is they function well as a team. Like Mary (8), they also work hard for the cause of Jesus, and Paul commends them for that.

We don't need to serve God alone.

The Bible commends teamwork and our interdependence on one another. By working together, Tryphena and Tryphosa likely accomplish more than they would if they worked apart. As a team, they can capitalize on the strengths of each other and cover each other's weaknesses.

Are we willing to work on a team, or do we seek to do things on our own?

[Discover more about Tryphena and Tryphosa in Romans 16:12.]

Persis

Paul affirms Persis as working hard for God. We don't know the details of why Paul says this, but he does. It's unlikely he commends her because of a single time when she worked hard but because of an ongoing lifestyle of diligent effort.

Her consistent history of hard work is the most probable reason why Paul includes Persis in his list of notable individuals. By doing so he extols her dedication in helping the cause of Jesus.

Her diligent labor to serve the Lord is all Paul needs to say. That's enough. May our lives be commendable, just like the life of Persis.

Though we shouldn't seek the approval of people, are we conducting ourselves in a manner worthy of praise or do our actions deserve criticism?

[Discover more about Persis in Romans 16:12.]

The Mother of Rufus

As Paul continues to wrap up his letter to the people in Rome, he tells them to greet Rufus and his mom too. Then Paul explains why he mentions her. She is like a mother to him.

We don't know if Paul's mom is alive or not. And if she is living, we don't know if they are on speaking terms, for she could have rejected him when he decided to follow Jesus. What we do know is when Paul needs a maternal figure in his life, Rufus's mom is there, caring for him as any good mom would do.

Regardless of our age or situation, we can be a spiritual parent to others. Do you know someone who needs a mom or a dad in their life?

[Discover more about Rufus's mom in Romans 16:13.]

Julia and the Sister of Nereus

Paul concludes his personal greetings at the end of his letter to the church in Rome by running through a list of names: Philologus, Julia, Nereus and his sister, and Olympas. He doesn't explain why these folks are important to him or worthy of mention, but they are.

This reminds me of someone receiving an award and giving an acceptance speech. Often we don't know why certain people are mentioned, but *they* do. Hearing their name in a public setting affirms their importance to the person receiving the award.

In the same way, Julia and the sister of Nereus are two women Paul publicly acknowledges. (The gender of Olympas is unclear.) Though we don't know why, Paul affirms these ladies' importance. For them this needs to be enough.

Sometimes what we do, even though extensive, may receive only passing mention—if any. May we accept such commendation, with the knowledge that God is fully aware of all the good we have done. His opinion is what matters most.

Are we willing to work hard even if we receive only passing praise for our efforts?

[Discover more about these women in Romans 16:15.]

The Wife of Cephas (Peter)

In the first letter Paul writes to the church in the city of Corinth, he goes into a bit of a rant about the expectations the Corinthian people place on him and their lack of support. As part of Paul's tirade, he implies Cephas (Peter) travels with his wife when visiting the various churches. While we know Peter is married, given that Jesus heals his mother-in-law, we know nothing about Mrs. Peter—except that she travels with him on his missionary journeys.

We don't know why she does this.

It may be it isn't safe for her to stay home alone—her husband's detractors could go after her. Perhaps she seeks adventure or likes to travel. Possibly the couple gets lonely when they're apart.

My preferred understanding is that she helps him in his work, that she's part of his ministry. Though he receives the recognition while she toils in anonymity, the important thing is that the church Jesus started grows.

How do we react when our spouse or close friend basks in the spotlight while we labor in the background? Are we happy for our role, or do we grow jealous and grumble?

[Discover more about Peter's wife in John 1:42 and 1 Corinthians 9:5.]

Nympha

In the letter Paul writes to the church in the city of Colossae, he asks them to pass along his greetings to the followers of Jesus in nearby Laodicea, especially to a woman named Nympha.

Why does Paul single out this lady and mention her by name? It might be because she has a house church. We don't know if she's the leader of this church, but we do know they meet in her home.

This implies she owns a large house—which is needed to accommodate everyone—and that she is generous with the things God has blessed her with. As a result, followers of Jesus have a place to meet.

God blesses each of us in diverse ways. How are we using what he has given us to help others and advance his kingdom?

[Discover more about Nympha in Colossians 4:15.]

Chloe

The Bible tells us nothing about Chloe, and only one verse mentions her by name. The issue is not about what she does as much as what happens in her household, those people under her authority.

Reports come to Paul, chiefly from Chloe's family, that the folks in the Corinthian church are quarreling with each other. They're fighting about doctrine. Sound familiar?

Particularly, the people align themselves with different teachers: Paul, Apollos, and Cephas (Peter), effectively dividing the church into factions and causing disunity. Others attempt to rise above the bickering by stating their focus is on Jesus. Still they mire themselves into the fray. They're part of the disharmony.

After calling them out, Paul goes into a lengthy teaching about this, ending with the encouragement for them to place their focus on God.

In doing all this, Paul neither commends nor condemns Chloe's family for taking the lead role in bringing this to his attention. On one hand, their actions are akin to gossip, something Paul repeatedly speaks against. After all, Paul is unlikely the only person who hears their tattling. Surely many other people hear their accusations too. On the other hand, Paul accepts their words as true and takes steps to address their concerns.

How much better it would have been for Chloe's household to not snitch on their fellow church members and instead seek to restore unity without involving others. Chloe, as the head of the house, could have directed her charges to act better. She should have led them well. Instead, she either makes no effort to guide them, or she lost her influence over them.

Do we seek to be peacemakers, or do we drag others into disagreements? Do we lead our families well or fail to lead them at all?

[Discover more about Chloe in 1 Corinthians 1:11–13.]

Claudia

As Paul wraps up his second letter to his protégé Timothy, some of Paul's associates add their greetings to his message. First there is Eubulus and then Pudens, who is followed by Linus. The fourth person named is Claudia, the only female of the group. But at least she's listed, for following her name comes a general greeting from everybody else. This is the only verse any of these four people appear in, so we know nothing else about them.

Why does Paul name four people and only indirectly refer to the rest of his associates? One explanation is that the quartet are simply nearby as he wraps up his letter. However, it's more likely they play a more critical role in the missionary work he leads. He recognizes their work by including their names in his letter, which is preserved for us to see today.

Claudia could be honored to be listed or she could be disappointed to appear fourth, but even so, she is listed. Others aren't.

Sometimes, like Claudia, we receive public recognition for the work we do. Other times we are identified only indirectly as part of a team. Sometimes we receive no acknowledgment for our efforts whatsoever.

From a human perspective, this matters a lot. We could become proud for being listed, annoyed that we weren't mentioned first, or angry that we received only a generic nod or no acknowledgment at all.

God's perspective is quite different. He desires that we work for him, not for an earthly reward—be it money, fame, or recognition—but for a heavenly one. Our reward will occur later when he says, "Well done! You're a good and faithful servant." And that should be enough. That *is* enough.

Do we sometimes do godly things for human rewards? Do we feel slighted when no one acknowledges our work?

[Discover more about Claudia in 2 Timothy 4:21. Also see Matthew 25:21.]

Euodia and Syntyche

Two women who work hard for the cause of Jesus are Euodia and Syntyche. Paul calls them his coworkers, for they struggled at his side to spread the good news about Jesus. Their actions are commendable, and it would be great to celebrate their diligent labor.

However, another trait—an unfortunate one—supersedes their work in advancing God's kingdom. They can't get along. Though they share a common goal, they live in disharmony with each other. They disagree. They argue.

Each one thinks she is right and the other, wrong. Both have too much pride to back down. Their interpersonal struggle affects those around them, hurting the common cause they work so hard to advance. Their bickering hurts Jesus's church.

Even though he isn't present, Paul must act.

He begs them to get along, to push through their spat and put it behind them. Notice that Paul doesn't take sides or try to mediate their dispute. He just tells them to work together and stop arguing. I hope they listen and do as Paul asks.

The work of God is important. However, despite our best efforts, we sometimes get in the way, thwarting the effectiveness of our work through petty squabbles and ungodly behavior.

Will we be commended for our work or criticized for arguing?

[Discover more about Euodia and Syntyche in Philippians 4:2–3.]

The Chosen Lady

John writes a letter to the elect, the chosen lady, along with her kids. Some people assume John uses an intimate metaphor to reference the church (the chosen lady) and its members (her children). But this interpretation falls apart because the New Testament considers the people as the church, not as two separate parts.

Rather, a literal understanding is that the chosen lady is an actual person. John's note is one of encouragement and instruction to someone he cares for deeply. Because the Bible preserves his letter for us, we can vicariously receive this same reassurance and teaching.

The chosen lady is a faithful follower of Jesus, and she, no doubt, desires to pass this on to her kids. She's likely a good mom, one who does her best to raise her children well. As a result, some of her kids are living good lives. But not all. Some pick up her legacy. Others do not.

She has done what she can to raise her kids right, but the decision of how they live their lives is up to them. John affirms her actions, but he doesn't hold her accountable for results outside of her control.

Whether we are parents of biological children or spiritual children, we need to do our best to raise our offspring well. Though we can't determine which path our kids take, we can point them in the right direction.

Are we doing all we can to guide those under our influence to follow Jesus?

[Discover more about the chosen lady in 2 John 1:1, 5.]

Jezebel (2)

The church in Thyatira has a problem. Her name is Jezebel.

Though she calls herself a prophet, she misleads people, encouraging them to pursue immoral behavior and act in unholy ways. She even advocates Satanism. Not only does Jesus promise a harsh punishment to her and her followers, he also criticizes those who tolerate her, allowing her errant teaching to go unchecked.

Tolerance of others is usually an act of love, a good thing to do. But sometimes tolerance is unacceptable, such as in the face of deviant teaching that encourages people to sin or leads them away from Jesus. This doesn't apply to differences of opinion or theological disputes. Those instances do demand tolerance. Acceptance is key.

However, we must speak against people who try to pull others from Jesus.

In what areas do we need to be more tolerant and accepting? Is there someone we must oppose because they speak against Jesus?

[Discover more about Jezebel in Revelation 2:18–29. Also see Luke 17:1–2.]

Everyone Has a Mom

Though the men in the Bible far outnumber the women, this isn't a reflection of God's priorities but of man's perversion of God's created order. Without these women, the biblical narrative would be much shorter and far less significant. Because of their lives and their actions, we are inspired, encouraged, motivated, and in a few cases, warned.

Beyond them and their example, we know that everyone in the Bible, both male and female, has a mom. These moms give birth to their children, nurture them, and usher them into adulthood. They mostly do this in obscurity. Nevertheless, without these moms giving life to their kids, we would not have their children to read about and learn from. Without these moms our understanding of God would be much different.

Last, you and I have a mom too. Along with our dad, we have her to thank for giving us life. She played a huge role in who we are today.

Have you thanked your mom for the gift of life? If she's no longer alive, perhaps you can write her a love letter of appreciation.

Thank you, Mom!

[Discover more about moms in Ephesians 6:2–3 and 1 Thessalonians 2:7–8.]

Bonus Material:
For Those New to the Bible

Each entry in this book ends with Bible references. These can guide you if you want to learn more. If you're not familiar with the Bible, here's a brief overview to get you started, give context, and minimize confusion.

First, the Bible is a collection of works written by various authors over several centuries. Think of the Bible as a diverse anthology of godly communication. It contains historical accounts, poetry, songs, letters of instruction and encouragement, messages from God sent through his representatives, and prophecies.

Most versions of the Bible have sixty-six books grouped in two sections: The Old Testament and the New Testament. The Old Testament has thirty-nine books that precede and anticipate Jesus. The New Testament includes twenty-seven books and covers Jesus's life and the work of his followers.

The reference notations in the Bible, such as Romans 3:23, are analogous to line numbers in a Shakespearean play. They serve as a study aid. Since the Bible is much longer and more complex than a play, its reference notations are more involved.

As already mentioned, the Bible is an amalgam of books, or writings, such as Genesis, Psalms, John, Acts, or 1 Peter. These are the names given to them, over time, based on the piece's author, audience, or purpose.

In the 1200s, each book was divided into chapters, such as Acts 2 or Psalm 23. In the 1500s, the chapters were further subdivided into verses, such as John 3:16. Let's use this as an example.

The name of the book (John) is first, followed by the chapter number (3), a colon, and then the verse number (16). Sometimes called a chapter-verse reference notation, this helps people quickly find a specific text, regardless of their version of the Bible.

Here's how to find a passage in the Bible based on its reference: Most Bibles have a table of contents, which gives the page number for the beginning of each book. Start there. Locate the book you want to read, and turn to that page. Then leaf forward to find the chapter you want. Last, skim that page to find the specific verse.

If you want to read online, just pop the entire reference, such as 2 Timothy 3:16, into a search engine, and you'll get lots of links to online resources. You can also go directly to BibleGateway.com or use the YouVersion app.

Although the intent was to place these chapter and verse divisions at logical breaks, they sometimes seem arbitrary. Therefore, it's a good practice to read what precedes and follows each passage you're studying since the text before or after it may hold relevant insight into the verses you're exploring.

Learn more about the greatest book ever written at ABibleADay.com, which has a Bible blog, summaries of the books of the Bible, a dictionary of Bible terms, Bible reading plans, and other resources.

Bonus Material: The Full Picture

A few women in this book may surprise some readers because they aren't in all versions of the Bible. They are:

- Susanna (1)
- Judith (2)
- Judith's maid
- Deborah (3)—Tobit's grandmother
- Sarah (2)—Tobias's wife

If these stories are new to you, consider them with an open mind. The accounts of these women are part of the Apocrypha. At the risk of oversimplifying something potentially contentious, here are four reasons why these women are included in this book:

1. Through much of Christianity's history, the Apocrypha has been part of the recognized Bible.

2. A slight majority of Christians today have the Apocrypha in their Bible.

3. The Apocrypha was included in the Septuagint, the Greek translation of the Old Testament, which was in use during Jesus's time. Jesus quoted from the Septuagint, and New Testament writers cited it in their work, which shows their acceptance of its contents.

4. The King James Version of the Bible originally included the Apocrypha, but those books were later removed. One commonly cited reason for this decision is that no Hebrew manuscripts of these books exist today, only their Greek versions.

The books in the Apocrypha are Tobit, Judith, 1 and 2 Maccabees, Wisdom, Sirach (also called Ecclesiasticus, not to be confused with Ecclesiastes), and Baruch, along with expanded passages for Daniel and Esther. (Other streams of Christianity include a few more books.)

These books of the Apocrypha either took place or were written in the few centuries prior to Jesus's birth, roughly covering a four-hundred-year time span. Some people call this period the silent years, claiming that God was silent, but the apocryphal books reveal God in action and show he wasn't silent at all.

I hope you enjoy reading about these women from the Bible's Apocrypha, but if the inclusion of their stories offends you, just skip these five ladies and read the rest of the book. Some of the versions of the Bible that include these books are The New Jerusalem Bible, Common English Bible (CEB), and New American Bible (NAB), among others.

Bonus Material:
For Further Study

The following women appear in the Bible, but they aren't covered in this book. These are left for you to investigate on your own. In approximate chronological order, they are:

Naamah (1), Lamech's daughter and sister of Tub-al-Cain: Genesis 4:19–22

Milkah (1), Nahor's wife (Nahor is Abraham's brother): Genesis 11:29, Genesis 22:20–23, and Genesis 24:15, 24, 47

Reumah, Nahor's concubine (Nahor is Abraham's brother): Genesis 22:23–24

Keturah, Abraham's concubine/second wife: Genesis 25:1, 4 and 1 Chronicles 1:32–33

Judith (1), one of Esau's wives: Genesis 26:34

Basemath (1), one of Esau's wives: Genesis 26:34 and Genesis 36:2–17

Mahalath (1), one of Esau's wives. She is also his first cousin, the daughter of his uncle Ishmael: Genesis 28:8–9

Adah (2), one of Esau's wives: Genesis 36:2–16

Timna, concubine of Esau's son Eliphaz: Genesis 36:12, 22 and 1 Chronicles 1:36, 39

Oholibamah, one of Esau's wives: Genesis 36:2–18

Elisheba, Aaron's wife and mother of the priests Nadab, Abihu, Eleazar, and Ithamar: Exodus 6:23

Mehetabel, the daughter of Matred and wife of King Hadad: Genesis 36:39 and 1 Chronicles 1:50

Serah, daughter of Asher: Genesis 46:17, Numbers 26:46, and 1 Chronicles 7:30

Shelomith (1), mother of a son who blasphemed God: Leviticus 24:11

Hammoleketh, mother of Ishhod, Abiezer, and Mahlah: 1 Chronicles 7:17–18

Abijah (1), the wife of Hezron, who gives birth to Ashhur after Hezron's death: 1 Chronicles 2:24

Atarah, wife of Jerahmeel and mother of Onam: 1 Chronicles 2:26

Abihail (1), wife of Abishur and mother of Ahban and Molid: 1 Chronicles 2:29

Shua, daughter of Heber and sister of Japhlet, Shomer and Hotham: 1 Chronicles 2:32

Maakah (1), Caleb's concubine: 1 Chronicles 2:48

Ephah, one of Caleb's concubines: 1 Chronicles 2:46

Maakah (2), sister of Makir: 1 Chronicles 7:15

Maakah (3), wife of Makir and mother of Peresh: 1 Chronicles 7:16

Maakah (4), the wife of Jeiel, 1 Chronicles 9:35

Sheerah, daughter of Beriah (or perhaps Ephraim), who built Lower and Upper Beth Horon as well as Uzzen Sheerah: 1 Chronicles 7:22–24

Baara, divorced wife of Shaharaim: 1 Chronicles 8:8

Hushim, divorced wife of Shaharaim: 1 Chronicles 8:8, 11

Hodesh, third wife of Shaharaim: 1 Chronicles 8:8–9

Maakah (5), wife of Gibeon: 1 Chronicles 8:29 and 1 Chronicles 9:35

Ahinoam (1), King Saul's wife and mother of his daughters Merab and Michal: 1 Samuel 14:50

Rizpah, King Saul's concubine, the daughter of Aiah and mother of Armoni and Mephibosheth: 2 Samuel 3:7 and 2 Samuel 21:7–14

Zeruiah (1), sister of David: 1 Chronicles 2:13–16

Abigail (1), sister of David: 1 Chronicles 2:13–16

Azubah (1), wife of Caleb: 1 Chronicles 2:18–19

Jerioth, wife/partner of Caleb: 1 Chronicles 2:18

Ahinoam (2) of Jezreel, one of David's wives: 1 Samuel 25:43, 1 Samuel 27:3, 1 Samuel 30:5, 2 Samuel 2:2, 2 Samuel 3:2, and 1 Chronicles 3:1

Abital, mother of Shephatiah, with David: 2 Samuel 3:2–4 and 1 Chronicles 3:3

Haggith, mother of Adonijah with David: 2 Samuel 3:2–4, 1 Kings 1:5–13, and 1 Chronicles 3:1–2

Eglah, wife of David and mother of Ithream: 2 Samuel 3:1–5 and 1 Chronicles 3:1–3

Maakah (6), one of King David's wives, daughter of Talmai (king of Geshur), and mother of Absalom: 2 Samuel 3:2–3 and 1 Chronicles 3:1–2

Abigail (3), daughter of Nahash and sister of Zeruiah the mother of Joab: 2 Samuel 17:25

Zeruiah (2), the mother of Joab: 2 Samuel 17:25

Shelomith (2), daughter of Zerubbabel: 1 Chronicles 3:19

Hazzelelponi, daughter of Etam: 1 Chronicles 4:3

Helah, one of Ashhur's two wives: 1 Chronicles 4:5

Naarah, one of Ashhur's two wives: 1 Chronicles 4:5–6

The Daughter of Pharaoh (2), Bithiah, who is married to Mered: 1 Chronicles 4:18

The Daughter of Pharaoh (3), Solomon also married a daughter of the Pharaoh: 1 Kings 3:1, 1 Kings 7:8, 1 Kings 9:16, 24, 1 Kings 11:1, and 2 Chronicles 8:11

WOMEN OF THE BIBLE

Basemath (2), daughter of Solomon, wife of Ahimaaz:
1 Kings 4:15

Taphath, King Solomon's daughter, married to
Ben-Abinadab: 1 Kings 4:11

Queen Tahpenes, Pharaoh's wife: 1 Kings 11:19–20

Zeruah, the mother of Jeroboam: 1 Kings 11:26

Zibiah, mother of King Joash: 2 Kings 12:1 and 2
Chronicles 24:1

Jehoaddan, mother of King Amaziah: 2 Kings 14:2 and
2 Chronicles 25:1

Jekoliah, mother of King Azariah (Uzziah): 2 Kings
15:1–2 and 2 Chronicles 26:3

Jerusha, daughter of Zadok and mother of King Jotham:
2 Kings 15:32–33 and 2 Chronicles 27:1

Queen Maakah (7), daughter of Abishalom, mother of
King Jeroboam, and grandmother of King Asa. She
was the queen mother for a while until Asa deposed
her for her pagan worship: 1 Kings 15:1–2, 9–13

Abihail (2), the daughter of Jesse's son Eliab, which
makes her King David's niece: 2 Chronicles 11:18

Naamah (2), an Ammonite who is King Rehoboam's
mother: 1 Kings 14:21 and 2 Chronicles 12:13

Mahalath (2), the wife of King Rehoboam. She
is King David's granddaughter and Jesse's

great-granddaughter on both her mother's and father's side (her parents were first cousins): 2 Chronicles 11:18

Azubah (2), the mother of King Jehoshaphat: 1 Kings 22:42 and 2 Chronicles 20:31

Abijah (2), mother of Hezekiah and daughter of Zechariah: 2 Kings 18:1–2 and 2 Chronicles 29:1

Hephzibah, mother of King Manasseh: 2 Kings 21:1

Meshullemeth, mother of King Amon: 2 Kings 21:19

Jedidah, mother of King Josiah: 2 Kings 22:1

Huldah, a prophet and wife of Shallum: 2 Kings 22:14–20 and 2 Chronicles 34:22–28

Zebidah, the mother of King Jehoiakim: 2 Kings 23:36

Nehushta, mother of King Jehoiachin: 2 Kings 24:8

Hamutal, mother of King Jehoahaz and King Zedekiah and daughter of Jeremiah: 2 Kings 23:31, 24:18, and Jeremiah 52:1

A Persian queen, wife of King Artaxerxes, who is present when Nehemiah asks permission to return to the city of Judea and rebuild it: Nehemiah 2:1–6

Anna (1), wife of Tobit: Tobit 1:9

Edna, Raguel's wife: Tobit 7:2

Antiochis, concubine of the king: 2 Maccabees 4:30

Apphia, a friend of Philemon and Paul: Philemon 1:2

Other considerations:

Prophetesses mentioned in the Bible:
- Miriam: Exodus 15:20
- Deborah: Judges 4:4
- Huldah: 2 Kings 22:14 and 2 Chronicles 34:22
- Noadiah: Nehemiah 6:14
- The prophetess, implicitly Isaiah's wife: Isaiah 8:2–3
- Anna: Luke 2:36
- Jezebel (2), a false prophet: Revelation 2:20

Virgin Daughter, as a proper name
- Virgin Daughter (my people): Jeremiah 14:17
- Virgin Daughter Zion: 2 Kings 19:21, Isaiah 37:22, and Lamentations 2:13
- Virgin Daughter Sidon: Isaiah 23:12
- Virgin Daughter Babylon: Isaiah 47:1
- Virgin Daughter Egypt: Jeremiah 46:11
- Virgin Daughter Judah: Lamentations 1:15

Woman in labor is a recurring image in the Bible, notably used by Isaiah and especially Jeremiah: Genesis 3:16, Psalm 48:6, Isaiah 13:8, Isaiah 21:3,

Jeremiah 4:31, Jeremiah 6:24, Jeremiah 13:21,
Jeremiah 22:23, Jeremiah 30:6, Jeremiah 48:41,
Jeremiah 49:22, Jeremiah 49:24, Jeremiah 50:43,
and Micah 4:9–10. Also see 1 Thessalonians 5:3.

Barren women are mentioned in Job 24:21, Proverbs
30:15–16, Isaiah 54:1, Galatians 4:27.

Ezekiel's prophetic parable about allegorical sisters
Oholah and Oholibah: Ezekiel 23:1–49

The mother of seven martyred sons: 2 Maccabees 7

The sisters of Jesus: Matthew 13:55–56 and Mark 6:3

Holy women of the past, unnamed women of whom
Sarah is an example: 1 Peter 3:5–6

A woman clothed with the sun, part of John's prophetic
vision: Revelation 12:1–17

The great prostitute, part of John's prophetic vision:
Revelation 17:1–18 and Revelation 19:2

Acknowledgments

I profoundly thank:

God who created us, both male and female, in his own image.

First readers Tim Gilbert and Sally Stap for your wise advice.

The members of Kalamazoo Christian Writers and Word Weavers of West Michigan for encouragement and support on this journey, along with many others who provided valuable feedback.

Shara Anjaynith Cazon, my steadfast assistant.

Joanna Penn for teaching me about publishing through her podcast and books.

And I'm especially grateful for each person who reads this book. May God inspire you through these words.

About Peter DeHaan

Peter DeHaan, PhD wants to change the world one word at a time. His books and blog posts discuss God, the Bible, and church, geared toward spiritual seekers and church dropouts. Many people feel church has let them down. Peter seeks to encourage them as they search for a place to belong.

But he's not afraid to ask tough questions or make religious people squirm. He's not trying to be provocative. Instead he seeks truth, even if it makes people uncomfortable. Peter urges Christians to push past the status quo and reexamine how they practice their faith in every area of their lives.

Peter earned his doctorate, awarded with high distinction, from Trinity College of the Bible and Theological Seminary. He lives with his wife in beautiful Southwest Michigan and wrangles crossword puzzles in his spare time.

A lifelong student of the Bible, Peter wrote the 700-page website ABibleADay.com to encourage people to explore the Bible, the greatest book ever written. His popular blog, at PeterDeHaan.com, addresses biblical spirituality, often with a postmodern twist.

Connect with him and learn more at PeterDeHaan. com.

Books by Peter DeHaan

Bible Bios series:

- *Women of the Bible: The Victorious, the Victims, the Virtuous, and the Vicious*

- *Friends and Foes of Jesus: Explore How People in the New Testament React to God's Good News*

52 Churches series:

- *52 Churches: A Yearlong Journey Encountering God, His Church, and Our Common Faith*

- *The 52 Churches Workbook: Becoming a Church that Matters*

- *More Than 52 Churches: The Journey Continues*

- *The More Than 52 Churches Workbook: Pursue Christian Community and Grow in Our Faith*

Dear Theophilus series:

- *Dear Theophilus: A 40-Day Devotional Exploring the Life of Jesus through the Gospel of Luke*

- *Dear Theophilus Acts: 40 Devotional Insights for Today's Church*

- *Dear Theophilus Isaiah: 40 Prophetic Insights about Jesus, Justice, and Gentiles*

- *Dear Theophilus Minor Prophets: 40 Prophetic Teachings about Unfaithfulness, Punishment, and Hope*

- *Dear Theophilus Job: 40 Insights About Moving from Despair to Deliverance*

Other books:

- *Jesus's Broken Church: Reimagine Our Sunday Traditions from a New Testament Perspective*

- *Woodpecker Wars: Celebrating the Spirituality of Everyday Life*

- *95 Tweets: Celebrating Martin Luther in the 21st Century*

- *How Big is Your Tent? A Call for Christian Unity, Tolerance, and Love*

If you liked *Women of the Bible*, please leave a review online. Your review will help other people discover this book and encourage them to read it too. That would be amazing.

Thank you.

Lightning Source UK Ltd.
Milton Keynes UK
UKHW020118230121
377551UK00003B/387